Abiding
IN HIS STRENGTH

Strengthened with all might,
according to his glorious power, unto all
patience and longsuffering with joy.
Colossians 1:11

GWEN WILKERSON
WITH BETTY SCHONAUER

FOREWORD BY NICKY CRUZ

Abiding In His Strength by Gwen Wilkerson

Copyright 2001 by David Wilkerson Publications, Inc.
P.O. Box 260, Lindale, TX 75771

ISBN 0-9709326-1-8

Expanded and edited by Carol B. Patterson

~ DEDICATION ~

TO MY WONDERFUL CHILDREN
AND GRANDCHILDREN:

DEBBIE AND ROGER JONKER
BRENT, MATTHEW AND TIFFANY

BONNIE AND ROGER HAYSLIP
BRANDON AND DAVID

GARY AND KELLY WILKERSON
DAVID ASHLEY, EVAN, ELLIOT AND ANNIE

GREG AND TERESA WILKERSON
ALYSSA AND RYAN

AND TO MY MOST CARING AND
WONDERFUL HUSBAND,
DAVID

IN MEMORY OF MY MOM AND DAD

~ CONTENTS ~

~ FOREWORD ~

BY NICKY CRUZ

Gwen Wilkerson had my respect before I ever met her. I was amazed when Dave told me that even as he was giving an altar call for those wanting new birth in Christ at the St. Nicholas Arena, his wife was ready to give birth any minute to their first son, Gary. I was one of the gang members at the arena who was born into the kingdom of God that night. Every wife wants her husband to be with her when she gives birth, and for Gwen to give her blessing for Dave to go to New York was one of the most touching acts of kindness I had ever witnessed. I am grateful to this day for the support Gwen gave Dave, and the personal sacrifice she made in allowing him to leave her alone to go through childbirth as he obeyed the Lord and held that rally that began the ministry he talks about in his book, *The Cross and the Switchblade*.

Not long after our conversions, Dave decided to take Israel Narvaez, another gang leader saved at St. Nicholas Arena, and me out to his home in Pennsylvania. As city boys, we had never been where there were more cows than people and although we had brand new hearts, we carried the street in our walk, talk, and dress. I wondered if Gwen knew what kind of "converts" Dave was bringing home. I was sure she'd never had anyone like us in her living room before.

As Israel and I walked into the little parsonage in Pennsylvania and saw Gwen coming to greet us, we carefully watched every nuance of her response to us, wondering if she would show fear, distrust or dislike. But from the moment I first met Gwen, I felt like I was being touched by tenderness and kindness. Without knowing me, she embraced me tightly and thanked God for my salvation, her eyes bright and full of love. Even though she was still very young, she was the first woman to demonstrate motherly love to me. I had a totally wrong impression of women because of my own mother's abuse and rejection. But Gwen was just the opposite. She was a lady—gracious, warm, and accepting. "Wow! These people are for real," we thought, as we saw her return our uneasiness with warm acceptance through her trusting eyes and endearing smile.

That evening Dave planned to visit someone in the church congregation. He turned to Gwen and asked, "Why don't you come with me? Nicky and Israel can stay with the children." For just a moment Gwen's eyes betrayed her surprise at his suggestion that these teenaged warlords—barely off the streets and a life of bloodshed and crime—should be left to care for her two precious pre-school daughters and her newborn son. She quickly recovered and gave us brief instructions on the care and feeding of three babies. But no one was more shocked than Israel and I at being entrusted with the responsibility of these children. And in response to that unprecedented trust, those babies were safer with us than they would have been with anyone else, because we literally would have protected them with our lives. As Gwen hugged us and walked out the door, I loved her more than I had ever loved anyone. In fact, my love and respect for her shaped and influenced my relationship with my wife, Gloria, and our four daughters.

This glimpse into Gwen's life at the inception of Dave's call to the gang members in New York City revealed what would become her ongoing role in his ministry. Many times she faced challenges, surprises, disappointments, and overwhelming situations as Dave's ministry unfolded and expanded. In her own strength, there was no way she could have been prepared. Only God knew what loomed ahead of her. But just as she rose to the challenge of having her home invaded by us, New York City street kids, through His strength she has met these challenges. During our week in Pennsylvania, Israel and I observed Gwen's serene and peaceful life—a loving family unit, a partnership. What we did not see was her future, rife with personal devastating illnesses, incomprehensible pain, and marital and emotional distress. But that is Gwen's story, and she tells it with great honesty and humility in this book.

Gwen has been faithful to her Lord Jesus, her husband, her children, her friends, and to those she and Dave have come to know through the ministries of Teen Challenge, World Challenge, and Times Square Church. One of Gwen's strongest characteristics is that she doesn't show people her pain. She is a woman of dignity who has learned to take her private life to the Lord. But through her own pain, God has given her an encompassing compassion that compels her to extend herself to others who are suffering.

Next to God, I believe Gwen is the greatest force in

David Wilkerson's life. She has been beside him in good times, bad times, times of nothing, and times of plenty. I believe God has preserved her life and continues to give her strength because Dave needs her.

Gloria and I are honored to give tribute to one of our heroes—a champion whose life is an example of God's grace in times of adversity. She has drunk deeply from the river of comfort the Holy Spirit has given, and allowed it to flow through her to others. And she has proven that our God "...comforteth us in all our tribulation, that we may be able to comfort them which are in any trouble, by the comfort wherewith we ourselves are comforted of God" (2 Corinthians 1:4).

~ INTRODUCTION ~

I was beginning to feel downright embarrassed. The woman before me was so much in earnest that I simply couldn't escape from her by anything short of physical flight. It was impossible for me to divert her and turn the conversation to a less disturbing channel.

We were standing in the auditorium of the Civic Center in Savannah, Georgia, where my husband had just addressed a crowd of some 1500 people. During the course of his talk on "Living a Life in Jesus Christ," David had shared some insights about marriage, getting most of his illustrations from our 24 years of life together. As often happens when David uses examples from our marriage, several of the women in the audience had sought me out after the benediction. I had become accustomed to having total strangers ask me such questions as, "Did he tell it like it *really* is, Gwen?" and "How did *you* feel about that?" But the woman who had me cornered now wasn't asking questions. She was *telling* me, in tones that could be heard several aisles away, "Gwen Wilkerson, *you* ought to write a book!"

Other folks had made that suggestion to me before, but always in a setting where I could simply brush it off by saying modestly, "Oh, no! One writer in the family is enough. I'll leave that job to David." This time the speaker's enthusiasm and volume had caught the attention of women standing nearby, and they began seconding the motion. I was barraged with a chorus of female voices exclaiming, "Yes, you should, Gwen"; "I think so, too"; "How about *your* version of things, Mrs. Wilkerson?"

Encouraged by their support, my persistent friend continued to press the point with great zeal. "A lot of other women have problems like the ones you've been through, Gwen. I'm sure you and David have worked out answers that are in harmony with the Lord's will, and we *all* would like to hear some of those answers." I stammered some vague reply and tried to make my escape. Before I succeeded, however, another woman stepped forward and pinned me down again. "Mrs. Wilkerson," she pleaded, "I for one would like to know more about your illnesses and about that time when you thought your marriage was washed up. If you *knew* how many of my Christian friends are on the brink of divorce after 20 or 30 years of marriage, and how many others have this morbid fear of cancer..."

The heads around us were nodding in obvious approval of each word she said. I tried to find a tactful way to tell them that I was the wrong person to come to for answers; I had no personal plan that guaranteed a successful marriage or a victorious Christian life. Didn't they know that we all have to find our own way by following the One who said *He* is the way?

Before I could phrase this answer, a petite young woman who had been quietly observing the scene summed up the comments of the crowd in one wistful statement: "I guess what we're saying is that we'd like to know if you've picked up any secrets along the way. If you *have*, please don't be selfish. Share the wealth!"

Touched by her plea, I smiled weakly and told them that I would "think about it." By then I was desperate to change the subject and get the attention away from me. Where was David, now that I needed him so badly? It was *his* suggestion that I accompany him on this ten-day tour of the Southeast. Why didn't he come to my rescue?

At that moment I spotted him standing just a few yards away. From the amused expression on his face, I knew that he had witnessed the entire episode and would not be my ally in escaping the situation. Stifling the impulse to stick my tongue out at him right there, I settled for giving him a "let's leave" look. At this point I wanted nothing more than to get back to the privacy of our hotel room.

Knowing how my husband felt about my writing a book, I wasn't eager to discuss the encounter with him— nor was I surprised when *he* brought up the subject as we were getting ready for bed.

"You see, Gwen," he began gently, "I haven't been kidding you when I told you that people are always asking me why you don't write a book. Now you've seen for yourself how interested women are in hearing about you and *your* life. Why don't you give it some thought?"

"Oh, Dave," I moaned, "we've been over all this before. You know how I feel. I'm no writer to begin with, and I'm too ordinary a person to have a book written *about* me. Who would want to read the story of my life? Just because I'm married to *you*—"

"That may be *part* of it, honey," David interposed quietly. "But the kinds of questions those women were asking you tonight weren't just out of curiosity about what it's like being married to David Wilkerson. Face it, Gwen. Most people *are* 'ordinary'; not every life is a gutter-to-glory story. And I know that you've walked long enough and closely enough with the Lord Jesus to have *something* important to share with other women."

"But not in a *book!*" I retorted. Then, seizing upon a fresh inspiration, I tried a diversionary tactic. "What gives with you, anyway? How many times have I heard you say there are too many books telling women how to run their lives, how to manipulate their husbands, how to find fulfillment? Why would you want *me* to jump on the bandwagon and try to tell women how to be ordinary Christians?"

With that, David shook his head and said with a laugh, "I give up, Gwen. You are impossible to reason with on this subject. I give you to the Lord. Argue it out with *Him* if you can. The logic of a female remains forever beyond me." Still chuckling, he gave me a good night kiss and turned out the light.

I had hoped that would be the end of the matter, and that my return home would find me content once more in my own niche as homemaker, wife, and mother. Certainly I didn't intend to entertain any more upsetting ideas about writing a book. It wasn't that I didn't want to be a witness for Jesus—and I didn't really think I had an inferiority complex, as David had sometimes suggested. But I *would* hate for anyone to think I regarded myself as somebody important or interesting enough to be the subject of a book; therefore, I had never before considered such a suggestion seriously—and I had never had

any guilt feelings about my failure to do so. Now, however, the peace I'd felt previously about this subject would
not return. That young woman's face as she pleaded,
"Don't be selfish; share the wealth," stayed in my mind
and her words pricked my conscience.

Finally, in desperation, I did as David suggested—tried
arguing it out with Jesus. And that was my big mistake! I
have learned over the years how to argue constructively
with my husband, but I now believe you cannot have a
really satisfying argument with the Lord. You do the arguing; *He* listens and loves you. You ask Him to tell you
what to do, and He counters by asking what *you* desire
for your life. Eventually I was reduced to admitting that I
did not really *know* what I wanted or needed, but that
my one desire was to follow His plan for my life—yes,
even if part of that plan was to let the reading public
know how He works in a life as ordinary as mine.

Somewhere in there I lost the argument, for this book
is being written. I do not know how it will "edify" the
reader, and I'm not at all convinced that someone else
can really learn from my mistakes. However, I am now
willing to trust all these questions to the Lord. If He
can use this story to help another woman with her own
Christian walk, I will be amazed but happy. All that follows has been committed to the illumination of the Holy
Spirit. For my part, I simply promise to "tell the truth,
the whole truth, and nothing but the truth"—to the best
of my memory.

Gwen Wilkerson

PART ONE

The Journey Begins

CHAPTER ONE

From the moment the old piano began rolling out the introductory chords, I knew what the first hymn of the morning was to be. I was only six years old, but I didn't have to turn to the correct page in the hymnal to recognize "Blessed Assurance." It was one of my favorites.

Mom and I always shared a songbook in church, but I knew *she* wouldn't need to see the words of this much-loved hymn. My mother really loved Jesus, and I loved to watch her face when she was singing about Him. *When I grow up I'm going to be just like her,* I thought, *and then I'll know for sure that "Jesus is mine," just the way Mom knows it now.*

The music rose to its fullest pitch as we reached the chorus: *"This is my story, this is my song, praising my Saviour all the day long."* I felt warm all over as I sang those words and listened to Mom's rich alto harmonizing with my childish soprano. Mom and I both loved gospel music. In that respect I was *already* like her.

As we began the second verse, I peeked around Mom to see what my older brothers were doing. David and

Ray didn't like Sundays as much as I did; maybe it was because they hated wearing neckties and coats. Standing stiffly between Mom and Dad with the hymnal open before them, they looked very bored with the whole business. I didn't understand boys. Just then I caught my father's disapproving gaze upon me. Hastily I turned my eyes to the front and sang even louder than before: *"Perfect submission, all is at rest, I in my Saviour am happy and blest."*

If I didn't understand David and Ray, I understood Daddy even less. He was always so solemn in his dealings with us. Mom said his strictness showed that he cared very much about us and wanted us to grow up properly, but sometimes it was hard for me to believe that. Even with Mom he was stern and demanding. No question about it: Daddy was the boss in our home, and his word was law. A few memorable spankings had convinced me once and for all of that important fact.

As the hymn ended, we sat back down on the hard, bench-like pew and I snuggled close to Mom to get more comfortable. Nature had not yet provided me with the cushion I needed to rest easy on that flat wooden seat. Once the singing was over, I began to lose interest in the service—but I always tried to behave as much like my mother as a six-year-old could. Whatever she did, I did. When she bowed her head, I bowed mine. When she sighed, "Thank you, Jesus!" I took that as my cue to whisper a soft "Amen." I was certain I'd never go wrong following in her footsteps.

During the sermon, however, I found it hard to listen

as attentively as she did. Pastor Casley talked for a long time that morning, and my thoughts soon began wandering. When he said something about the hardships many of our members were suffering because of the Depression, I began to wonder again just what this "depression" business was all about. The year was 1937, and we'd been having a depression for as long as I could remember. I often heard the grown-ups say that our little town of Forest Hills—located in the mountainous coal-mining region around Pittsburgh—had been hit pretty hard. Several stores had closed down for lack of business, and Mom told me that a lot of men were out of work. She said we should be thankful that Daddy had a good job at Westinghouse and he had been there so long that they couldn't lay him off. He had started working there when he was 14, and his first job was sweeping floors. Now he had a job in management. "Your father is a good provider," Mom proudly assured us.

So I guess we weren't poor. It just seemed that way sometimes because we children had to account for every penny we spent. Our home, although comfortably furnished, was lacking in frills or luxuries. Dad himself did the grocery shopping and would go miles out of his way to save a few pennies. Mom prepared good, nourishing meals with the "bargain" foods Dad brought home.

He's just plain strict about everything, I thought. *He never lets us have fun the way other people do.*

At that moment I was thinking that "fun" might be something like going to a skating rink or a movie. Such frivolous activities were not allowed by my father or by our church. Until I started school and met kids from other backgrounds, I hadn't known what I was missing. Soon I was beginning to find out there was more to life than going to church and helping Mom with the housework. I knew better than to admit that I had a desire for "forbidden fruit," but I did feel cheated sometimes when my friends told me they felt sorry for me. It was even worse when I overheard remarks to the effect that Gwendolyn Carosso was *different*.

Being the only daughter in our family had its drawbacks, too. Since Mom and I were such good friends, I didn't really *mind* helping her with the housework (even though I hated ironing my father's and brothers' shirts), but it seemed to me that my brothers had more fun than I did. David and Ray could play baseball and football, but until they reached high school I wasn't even allowed to go watch their games. Daddy was really fussy about where I went and who went with me. About the only place he allowed me to go without question was to the church. I was glad our church had so many activities for kids.

Of course there *were* a few advantages to being Daddy's little girl. For one thing, when my brothers started teasing me—and they did their share of teasing—I only had to shed a few feminine tears to get them in trouble with Dad. For another, I had attractive dresses to wear to Sunday school and church—the only pretty items in our otherwise drab environment. My brothers' clothes were bought to be serviceable; mine were selected with an eye to looks as well as practicality. *Being a girl isn't so bad after all,* I decided.

Mom's loud "Amen!" startled me and reminded me that we were in church. After a final hymn, Pastor Casley pronounced the benediction and the service was over. Dad herded us out the door and into his 1935 Ford as quickly as possible. He was anxious to get to Grandma Morgan's house for Sunday dinner. That was the pattern our family had followed as long as I could remember. Sundays were always the same.

A few years later, just after I had turned ten, there came a Sunday that *wasn't* the same. That was the Sunday I was baptized. Somewhere in those years I had decided not to wait until I was *all* grown up to follow Jesus. My Sunday school teachers had convinced me that I could begin that journey whenever I decided to let Jesus come into my heart. With my mother's encouragement and my pastor's counsel, I publicly declared my faith and was deemed ready for baptism. I can still clearly recall how strange the white robe felt to me as I stood before the congregation and answered the questions put to me. Vivid in my memory also is the shock I received when the pastor immersed me gently but firmly in the chilly water of the baptistry. I was too young to have a complete theology all worked out, and I wasn't too clear on a lot of doctrine. What I did know was that Jesus loved me, had died to save me, and wanted to live in me. I wanted that, too.

In the years that followed—partly because I *did* love the Lord and partly because my opportunities for approved recreation were so limited—the church occupied a more and more important place in my life. Sunday school, church services, church dinners, picnics and, later, choir practice and youth fellowship activities were my only social outlets. I couldn't go to dances and parties, but I had frequent opportunities to get together with my friends at church. I drew very close to these young people in my teen years.

In that close fellowship I had a most significant experience as a teenager. After the church service one Sunday evening, three of us lingered at the altar railing to seek the infilling of the Holy Spirit. Jesus chose that time to give all of us the "second touch" that He promised to His followers just before His ascension. Because of my mother's life and our church's teaching, I knew that the Holy Spirit could be personally experienced as a reality, but I was not at all prepared for the overflowing joy and love that came to me with that experience. Ever since that time I have shared my mother's "blessed assurance" that Jesus *is* mine and He has given me His Holy Spirit as a "foretaste of glory divine." That assurance has sustained me throughout my life.

The love of music that I first discovered in singing hymns at my mother's side also found expression within the church. After a few years of piano lessons, I was able to accompany the hymn-singing in Sunday school and at our youth fellowship. Making music was okay with Dad, as long as it was the right *kind* of music.

No one told me that rebellion is supposed to be an integral part of the teen years, and I seem to have grown up without causing my parents any serious concern. I'm sure I must have pouted a bit over the fact that I *always* had to wear modestly long skirts, instead of the slacks and shorts that my friends often wore. I recall borrowing my best friend's lipstick in the girls' room of our high school, where Dad's disapproving eye could not follow.

Deep inside, however, I knew that the rules and regulations imposed by my family and our church—rules that seemed so harsh and unfair at times—were based on genuine love for me and a desire to help me remain faithful to the Lord I had chosen to serve. It is pretty hard to rebel against that kind of love.

I can recall only one time when Dad's convictions concerning what was right and what was wrong for me were at serious odds with my own ideas. From the time I was in junior high, I liked to fuss with my hair and give home permanents to neighbors and friends. I felt certain that I would make a good beautician if I could get some training after I finished high school. Dad would not even consider such a plan. *His* daughter playing on the vanity of other women for money? The mere idea was revolting to his sober temperament. He said one absolute and final NO and refused to discuss the matter ever again.

I continued to toy with the notion for a while, though I doubt seriously that I would ever have acted in direct opposition to his wishes. Still, a career as a beautician was something I might enter into—someday, but the "someday" of those dreams never came. In my early teens there was born another dream, which eventually supplanted all other desires. You see, I was only 13 when I first met David Wilkerson.

David

❧

"Grandma, come here a minute! I want to show you something." I didn't dare call too loudly. Grandma's house was set so close to her daughter's home next door that I was sure the occupants could hear me if I yelled. From where I was standing—just out of their view—I could see a large portion of Aunt Marion's dining room. I felt a shiver of excitement run through me.

"Hurry, Grandma! You'll miss him!"

"Miss *who,* child? What's all the fuss about?" my grandmother demanded as she hastened to join me at the window.

"Don't stand *there,* Grandma. Come over here by me. I want you to see this boy at Aunt Marion's."

"Oh, *him!* The skinny one? That's Pastor Wilkerson's son, isn't it? Their oldest boy. What about him?"

"Well, Grandma," I sighed, trying my best to sound dramatic, "someday I am going to marry him. That's my future husband!"

"My goodness, child! You do have grown-up ideas, don't you?" Grandma was trying not to laugh at me, but she was losing the battle. "How old is he? Not more than 13, I'll bet—same as you—and neither of you dry behind the ears. You'd better not rush into it just yet. Your mother and father might have something to say about it, you know."

In spite of myself, I began chuckling with her. It did sound ridiculous. I'd never been interested in boys, and I certainly was not allowed to date. But some inner voice, some quiet conviction born in me that day told me that Pastor Wilkerson's oldest son would one day be my husband. It was a conviction that would not go away.

The Wilkerson family was having Sunday dinner at Aunt Marion's, after Pastor Wilkerson had preached a "trial sermon" at the Turtle Creek Church—our church. It was clear to me from the first that he would be called to serve as our new minister, and I was ecstatic about it. Both Mr. and Mrs. Wilkerson were ordained ministers, and our morning service had been lively and inspired. David had an older sister, Juanita; a younger sister, Ruth; and two younger brothers, Jerry and Donald. I felt sure there were good days ahead for our church, and the notion persisted that there were good days ahead for *me*.

David was not the average teenager. Perhaps having not one but *two* parents who were ministers is what made him somewhat different. Whatever the reason, he was, from the time I first met him, a young man with a clear calling from God. Already he knew that he was set apart to be a preacher of the gospel. Consequently, he spent his spare time reading the Bible, writing sermons, and preaching—starting at the age of 14—in nearby communities when a minister was absent. The intensity of his faith awed me.

It must have been David's spiritual qualities that I found so irresistible, because it certainly wasn't his looks. To begin with, he was too skinny and his sandy hair was too unruly. Except for his startlingly blue eyes, there was nothing about his physical appearance that I found especially attractive. Nevertheless, after seeing him from Grandma's window, I never really looked at another boy. I made up my mind that I was destined to be a minister's wife.

From that time on, I spent most of my teenaged energies keeping an eye on my future. It was no easy matter to become David's girl. I was not at all the pushy type. And even if I had been, there was really no way to push, since my father didn't allow me to date until I was through high school. But since I *could* take part in all church-related group activities, David and I were together several times each week. We didn't attempt to pair off, but I kept an eagle eye on him. By the time we were juniors in high school, David could be counted on to offer me a ride home from church events.

Gradually everyone, even David, began to think of us as a twosome. Whether this was the result of mutual attraction or of my persistence, I remain afraid to ask. But by the time we graduated from high school in 1950, he was as committed to a future which included me as I was to being a minister's wife—David's wife. We just seemed right for each other. We saw our relationship as part of God's plan for our lives.

We may have felt that God was bringing us together, but Dad thought otherwise. In spite of David's obvious sobriety and his willingness to work hard (he kept one or more part-time jobs all during high school), my father considered him a poor prospect for marriage. Dad himself had arrived at success the hard way. He didn't feel that a country preacher would be as reliable a breadwinner as he had become and he didn't want me to settle for a lower standard of living.

Surprisingly enough, Dad never forbade me to see David—a fact that probably says more about the obvious seriousness of my intentions than it does about any softening on my father's part. He must have known that he could not change my mind, so sure was I that David was "Mr. Right" for me. But that didn't stop him from trying. He'd point out that David never had time to take me any place, and that his courting left a lot to be desired—all of which was true.

After graduating from high school, David spent nine months at Central Bible College in Springfield, Missouri. When he came home on weekends or holidays, he was either filling vacant pulpits in the communities around Pittsburgh or working at one of his numerous wage-earning activities. He was not able to be the most attentive of beaus.

No doubt Dad's needling and his outright encouragement to look around for other prospects led me to accept the only other date I can recall having. It happened in the summer after David returned from Bible school. His rival was a polite, attentive, and moderately well-to-do young man whose only obvious drawback was that he wasn't David. Nevertheless, he had the built-in attribute of making Mr. Wilkerson sit up and take notice. David, I had decided, took our relationship a bit too much for granted. The night I had my date with this new beau, I saw David's green jalopy circling our block time and again. I didn't really enjoy the evening very much, but I did take a wicked delight in watching David fume.

The following Christmas David and I became officially engaged. From his earnings at Hawkins Market and as a used-car salesman, David was somehow able to scrape together enough to buy me a small diamond solitaire as a Christmas gift. My dream, begun nearly eight years earlier, was actually coming true! I was going to be David's wife.

We set our sights on a wedding in June. Since my graduation from high school I had been working at Lawson's Manufacturing Company in nearby Wilkinsburg. Now I began saving every penny I could for a wedding dress. David continued his supply preaching on weekends and worked at all the part-time jobs he could manage. Consequently, we didn't have much time to spend together during our engagement. I began to accompany him to his Sunday services, just so I could be with him during the rides to and from the town where he was preaching. About the only times we were ever alone before our wedding were on those Sunday trips. I wonder now if it ever crossed my mind that I had a lot to learn about this man I was going to marry, and about marriage itself. David and I had practically grown up together and had been rather set on marriage since high school, but our dates had almost always been in the presence of others. Although I knew David was a warmly affectionate man, our relationship had scant opportunity to get beyond the hand-holding stage. I had learned much of value from my mother—but sex education was not included. Consequently, I was as naïve and uninformed as it was possible for a young woman to be in the latter half of the twentieth century. David was scarcely more sophisticated. We were in love, but we maintained a gingerly respectful relationship until our wedding day.

I also wonder if I had any idea how much growing up I would have to do in the years that lay ahead. Life with a country preacher must have seemed safe and predictable. How could I guess at the calling this man was to receive? How could I imagine the extent to which I would be stretched into new roles, new spiritual understandings? I only knew that I was going to marry a minister, and that my life would be to share David's life.

What More Could We Want?

❧

CHAPTER THREE

David and I were married by his father on June 14, 1952, in the same Turtle Creek Church where our courtship had begun. It was a modest ceremony, with just our families and close friends in attendance, but it seemed to me a perfect beginning for our life together. The solemn vows taken in the sight of God echoed the seriousness of our commitment to each other and to our Lord. And the reception that followed, in a hall over the local bank, was an occasion of joy and fellowship. Even Dad had relented sufficiently to participate willingly in the ceremony. If I was to be given in marriage—even to a minister with a dubious financial future—he was the one to give me away. I was, after all, his little girl.

Our photographer somehow got confused and never showed up, but a friend with a camera managed to capture the bride and groom for posterity with a single snap of the shutter. That photograph, enlarged and framed, hangs today on our bedroom wall—a faded reminder of a vividly memorable day. Our impossibly long courtship was over and our future belonged together. I felt that our marriage was off to a good start.

At least I felt that way until after we left the reception amidst the traditional shower of rice and the clatter of tin cans tied to the bumper of David's green Edsel. By then the hour was late and our destination was not quite clear. We planned to spend our honeymoon week in the Washington, D.C. area, but David had neglected to secure any hotel reservations for that first night. Consequently our wedding night was spent in a tiny Maryland town, in a hotel which surely has collapsed from age by now. The setting could hardly be called romantic. A naked light bulb hung from the cracked ceiling of our sparsely furnished room. It was fortunate that neither of us was accustomed to luxury, and even more fortunate that both of us had a sense of humor and were very much in love.

Love won the day, and eventually, the whole week. Even David's severe case of sunburn (acquired at the pool of the motel where we spent the rest of the week) and my case of bride's nerves could not rob us of the joy of being together as husband and wife. Our honeymoon was not a storybook week of bliss, but it was a good introductory course to all we had to learn about each other, and about this whole business of marriage.

Back home again, we moved into a one-room apartment on the third floor of the Wilkersons' home. One room was all we needed at that point, because we were out of town more than we were at home. David was now spending his full time as a traveling evangelist, and his new bride was only too happy to accompany him on his trips. Dad's predictions about the uncertainty of our financial situation were proving to be accurate, since David's only income was from love offerings given when he preached. We were totally dependent upon God's providence for all our material needs.

The Lord met those needs beautifully. We were well fed by the church people in whose homes we stayed on our tours, and the money received from the offerings covered our other small expenses: gasoline for the car and rent at the Wilkersons'. We were more than satisfied with our lot. We were together, and we were doing the Lord's work. David was preaching the gospel as only he could preach it, and was gaining valuable experience in evangelism. I was learning to be his helpmate and companion in life. What more could we possibly want?

Well, ready or not, more was coming. Before we had celebrated our first anniversary, I discovered that I was carrying a child. Although we hadn't planned to become parents so soon, I found myself excited and pleased. It was fortunate that I welcomed the prospect of motherhood, because my pregnancy necessitated some *un*welcome changes in our way of living. With a baby on the way, extensive traveling no longer seemed wise for me. Consequently, David continued his itinerant ministry alone, while I sat at home awaiting the baby's birth. Taking it easy, watching my diet, and getting plenty of sleep somehow didn't seem nearly so important or satisfying as the work David was doing. I felt left out of things and began to experience twinges of envy and depression.

These thoughts remained hidden ones. I could scarcely acknowledge them to myself—much less tell anyone else that I was jealous of my own husband. Those close to me probably attributed my unaccustomed peevishness to my "delicate condition," but Jesus knew the real reason for my moods. When I turned to Him in prayer, He tried to minister His comfort to me. He assured me that I was doing His work just as much as David was. Creating new life is one of His greatest pleasures and I was His instrument in this particular bit of creation. He tried to show me that my job and David's were going to be different in style, but not in quality. Eventually the joy of anticipation overcame resentment. But the final lesson was not to be learned in one sitting.

As the time drew near for our baby's birth, I was glad the Lord was so close at hand, because it grew increasingly evident that David might *not* be. He tried to plan his preaching missions so that he could be with me when the baby was born, but the due date came and went with no sign of labor. When a full week passed, David had to return to his travels in order to meet some commitments made months earlier. He called home every night and came home as often as possible—but he was not with me on October 4, 1953, when Deborah Ann came into the world. Once she decided to make her appearance, she was very cooperative about the whole process—and she was so beautiful that I found it easy to forgive her for all the frustration and anxiety she had caused David and me by her reluctance to be born. She weighed in at eight pounds and had a head full of light brown, curly hair. I decided to keep her.

When David arrived home to greet his new daughter,

he immediately fell under her spell, too. I had never seen him happier or prouder. How could I be angry with a guy who was so obviously pleased with me? The disappointment I'd felt because he wasn't with me at such an important time was pushed aside, and we simply rejoiced together in the wonderful gift of new life.

Mothering came easily to me. I loved caring for Debbie, and once again I felt useful and productive. As soon as she was old enough to travel, David insisted that the three of us hit the trail together. I was delighted! Despite the inconvenience of diapers and bottles, and the sometimes wearisome aspects of being perpetual guests in other people's homes, it felt good to be back on the road with my husband and once more a visible part of his life.

It was David who brought this phase of our marriage to an end near the time of Debbie's first birthday. He broke the news to me as we were driving home after a particularly successful preaching mission.

"Gwen, honey," he began, "I think the Lord has something else He wants me to do now. I believe He's calling me to be the pastor of a church—you know, like Dad and Mom."

I held my breath, afraid of acting too hopeful. I didn't want David to divert his gifts to a stationary ministry just because of the baby and me, but I couldn't suppress the feeling of excitement that was rising within me. A church ministry would mean a more normal life together and a home of our own. Trying to sound casual, I replied, "Well, that's interesting, David—but I thought you felt your calling was to be an evangelist."

"Well, yes," David acknowledged. "I mean, that's what I've been doing for the past several years, and I think God has honored the work. But just now, I think He has something else in mind. Let's pray about it—OK?" And pray we did.

When the answer came, David's hunch proved accurate. He received a call to serve a rural church in Philipsburg, Pennsylvania, and we quickly settled into the routine of a country pastor's family.

The next four years were among the happiest of my life. They were growing years for us and for the church. The people of our small congregation were wonderful, warm folks who did everything they could to make us feel at home. David's ministry seemed especially effective during this time. He never lost his evangelistic fervor, but to his preaching skills God now added the special gifts of a pastor. The result was a rapidly growing church. Within a year, the 70-member congregation had almost tripled in size and we had a new church building and a new parsonage. Clearly the Lord was blessing this congregation with growth and prosperity.

He was also blessing our family with increase. On March 8, 1955, a second daughter arrived on the scene, bringing added joy to our lives and companionship to 18-month-old Debbie. This time David was in town—but if I had envisioned my husband's hand in mine and his voice giving me encouragement as I labored, I had the wrong fellow in mind. David was so nervous that he had to leave the hospital to take a walk and pray while Bonnie Kay was coming into the world. His prayers must have been heard, for the Lord gave her a safe passage and gave us another beautiful baby girl. With her dark eyes and cap of dark ringlets, she made a pretty contrast to her blond sister. We felt blessed to have two such beautiful and healthy daughters.

During the Philipsburg years, David and I had time to learn about being parents. We discovered, through experience, how to administer the discipline we both wanted for our children with equal parts of firmness and love. We dedicated both girls to God in infancy and claimed His promises for them from the time they were born. As we began to see His hand on their lives, we were able to relax and trust His ability and willingness to compensate for our shortcomings as parents.

I would have been willing to spend a lifetime in Philipsburg, in the quiet stream of fellowship and contentment we found there. I could picture David and me growing older in that tranquil little town and watching our children grow up, marry, and have children of their own.

The picture was an appealing one, but my vision was shortsighted. Although such peaceful times might eventually come, the Lord had other jobs for us to do in the meanwhile. We had many lessons yet to learn at His hand. Philipsburg was just a starting point, a training ground for both David and me. We were soon to know new labors for the Lord.

A Couple of Fleeces

"What's the matter, Dave?" I asked for the tenth time in as many days. For weeks my husband had been acting unnaturally, and I knew something was bothering him. He had been spending late hours slumped before the TV set, staring vacantly at the screen. It simply wasn't like him to remain idle so much of the time.

"Oh, nothing, honey," was the reply he most frequently gave me. This time, however, he jumped up, began to pace back and forth, and said, "Gwen, honey—I don't know!" He shook his head in bewilderment. "There's something the Lord wants me to do but I can't seem to get a handle on it. I feel like He's getting me ready for something and it makes me restless not knowing where I'm heading. I'm sorry." He reached out to pat me on the shoulder. "I don't mean to take it out on you and the girls. I just can't relax until I find out whatever it is He wants me to hear."

My response was more sarcastic than understanding: "Well, you might start by turning the volume down on the TV, so you can hear Him when He speaks."

David turned and stared at the set, obviously seeing and hearing it for the first time. "Oh—right!" he said, as he stepped over and snapped it off. "Guess I *have* been spending a little too much time with the tube lately. I just can't seem to concentrate."

His confusion was as unusual as the rest of his behavior had been lately. I'd never seen David quite like this—so distracted and distant. Usually his instructions from the Lord seemed to come to him clearly and directly. One of the things I most admired in him was his ability to perceive the direction the Lord was taking in his life and to act accordingly. Now he seemed to be completely at sea. Since I was obviously being no help, I gave him a hug and told him I was going to bed. Before the bedroom door closed, I heard the TV click back on and the sound of The Late Show once more filled the house. My sympathy for David struggled with my feelings of annoyance.

The next day David astounded me by announcing that he was selling the television set.

"You're *what?*" I asked incredulously. "How on earth will you entertain yourself when the rest of us are asleep if you sell the TV?"

I didn't mind at all parting with the TV if it meant regaining a normal husband—but I suspected that getting rid of the television wasn't the whole answer. David, however, was hustling around looking for paper and pencil and talking about a "fleece."

I thought I understood the purpose of fleeces. I knew all about Gideon in the Old Testament, and how he asked the Lord to confirm His promise of help in battle by causing a fleece spread on the ground overnight to become either wet or dry, according to Gideon's request. But I couldn't see what that had to do with selling our television set. David had already decided to sell it. What was he asking the Lord to tell him?

"Well, Gwen," David explained as he sharpened the pencil he found, "I think the Lord wants me to spend more time in prayer and less time watching TV, but I'm not *sure* of anything these days. Maybe I'm making a big fuss about nothing. Maybe the television set should stay right here and I should learn to watch it less. I don't know. Anyway, I'm going to write a want ad for the paper and ask the Lord to accept it as a fleece. If He wants me to spend those late-night hours praying instead of watching TV, He'll show me by sending a buyer to purchase our set—and sending him within a half-hour after we receive our paper with the ad in it."

"Half an hour!" I hooted. "Why, Dave Wilkerson, I don't think you *want* to sell that TV set at all! Why not give it at least a day or two? Half an hour is impossible!"

"But you see, Gwen, that's just it." David was perfectly serious. "I want to make it *almost* impossible, so that I can be sure it's the Lord who's doing it. If we have a buyer that fast, I'll know that God engineered the whole thing and I'll have my answer."

In spite of my skepticism, I felt a stirring of anticipation as he mailed the advertisement, and I could hardly wait for it to appear in the paper.

Two days later, the paper containing David's ad was placed in our mailbox at 8 A.M. After checking it for accuracy, we sat in the living room with our girls and watched the clock. As each minute slid by, I could see David growing more restless. Debbie and Bonnie thought it was a funny game, but David wasn't laughing. When 29 minutes had passed, he opened his mouth to say something. But he never had a chance. The phone rang at that moment and the TV was sold—just like that! David had his answer, and we were once again impressed with the unusual measures our Lord employs to communicate with His children who are willing to hear Him.

Now David had ample time for prayer and meditation, and I no longer felt that a mechanical picture device was my rival for his attention. I hoped he would soon have some real guidance as to what the Lord wanted him to do next. But when the guidance came, I began to think we should have kept the television set.

"Gwen, I'm going to have to make a trip to New York City," David announced one morning at breakfast. "Do you mind? I should be back within a couple of days."

Did I mind? Well, not exactly. I knew David well enough to trust him, even in that big city. But I did want to have some idea as to why he suddenly had to visit a place 350 miles away.

"Look at this," David commanded by way of explanation. He spread before me an open copy of *Life* magazine, and I found myself looking reluctantly at an artist's drawing of seven teenaged youths who were being tried for murdering a crippled boy, Michael Farmer. I still didn't understand what this had to do with David's decision to go to New York, and I told him so.

"Well, I can't look at those faces without being terribly

moved," was David's response. "The Lord seems to be calling me to help them in some way. I have no idea what I can *do,* but I know I have to go to New York and try to see them."

At prayer meeting that Wednesday night, David brought his burden of concern before the congregation. Encouraged by their support—expressed tangibly in the free-will offering they gave for his trip—he and our youth director, Miles Hoover, started out for New York the next morning. Although he went with my blessing, I was secretly afraid that he might have misunderstood what the Lord wanted him to do.

The rest is history: his being thrown out of the courtroom by the police, the news wire photograph that showed him wildly waving his Bible, and the way papers all over the country picked up the story of the preacher who had disrupted the Michael Farmer trial.

After leaving New York on Friday evening, David and Miles drove to Scranton, where David's parents were now living. They visited with them briefly, and then came on to Philipsburg Saturday afternoon to face the music.

I'd been fielding phone calls ever since the papers had been delivered that day, but I still didn't know exactly what had happened. I did know that David hadn't gone to New York to get his picture in the paper. I figured I'd have to hear the explanation from David himself. But when he got home, he could hardly talk about what had happened, even to me. He was confused by the strange turn of events, and dreaded going before his congregation on Sunday with nothing positive to report.

"Gwen, I've made a real mess of things," was his weary summation of the events. "I never got to talk to even one of those kids. All I did was bring my ministry to public ridicule. And *still* I feel that the Lord wants me involved with those boys in some way. Am I crazy or something? What am I going to tell the congregation?"

I didn't know. So I asked, "What did your folks suggest?"

"Well, Mom thinks the Lord may have a purpose in all this. I can't see it, but I *do* keep thinking of that verse in Romans about all things working together for good to those who love the Lord."

It was some time before we discovered that the Lord did indeed have a purpose in the public humiliation David had suffered. When he gained the courage to return to New York in response to the Lord's persistent direction, doors for ministering to the youthful members of other street gangs were opened, precisely *because* David had become known as the "skinny preacher who got himself thrown out of court by the police." We marveled anew at the Lord's planning and His perfect timing.

In the meanwhile, however, David's pride was being severely bruised, and I could do little to help him. In fact, I had about all I could handle myself. I was expecting our third child, and was not feeling as well as I had during my first two pregnancies. David was making increasingly frequent trips to the city, walking the streets and trying to follow the Lord's leading. His absences meant that I was having to handle a lot of the midweek calls that came in from parishioners. Debbie, four-and-a-half, and Bonnie, three, still demanded a lot of my time and energies. In spite of my deep concern for David, who was growing even more gaunt than usual, I could do little to help him except love him and pray for him.

As the birth of the baby became imminent, my concern for David gradually gave way to annoyance at his frequent and prolonged absences from home. When I needed him most, he was off chasing after a bunch of unknown gang members in a city miles away. *What about us?* I'd ask myself and the Lord. *What about his own children? What about me? Don't* we *matter at all? Why isn't he here taking care of his church and his family?*

The jealousy and anger I'd experienced before Debbie's birth were mild compared to the emotions now seething inside me and sometimes boiling over. I had not dealt with them adequately when they attacked me the first time. Now they had returned in force and my control was weaker.

The more I indulged in self-pity, the more irritable I became. One Friday night when I was expecting David home, I deliberately locked him out just to teach him a lesson of some kind. Of course I couldn't sleep and had to get up to let him in when I heard him at the door. But I hoped my childish behavior had made a point.

David was in New York holding a series of evangelistic rallies for gang members at St. Nick's Arena when Gary Randall was born. I was so relieved that the long ordeal of this pregnancy was finally over (Gary, like Debbie, was a slowpoke about getting here), and so thankful to have a healthy son that the bitterness I'd been harboring over the preceding weeks just seemed to evaporate. *No sense weeping over the past,* I told myself. *It's all over now. David couldn't be here, and that's that. Probably the pregnancy was what made you so irritable. Things will be fine now. Everything is great!*

And everything *did* seem wonderful again. David was home for a long stay and was beaming with pride over his son. As I recovered my strength, my normal balance and even disposition also returned. When David told me about another birth that had occurred almost simultaneously with Gary's, I knew once more that God was controlling *all* the events of our lives.

On the night of Gary's birth, David had been trying to share God's love with a homeless young gang leader named Jo-Jo. Jo-Jo had never known any kind of love and he found it hard to believe David's assurances that God loved him and cared about him. When he heard that I was soon to have a baby and that David wanted a boy, he made what was for him a huge step toward faith. He asked God to prove that He loved him by giving us a son.

Jo-Jo was honestly seeking God, and his prayer was as much a genuine "fleece" as David's test with the TV had been. Gary's birth convinced Jo-Jo that God *does* love him and that He answers prayer. That very night a new life was born in Jo-Jo—a life that was to bear much fruit. But that's another story!

The St. Nick's rallies led to tremendous breakthroughs in the lives of some of the other gang leaders David had been working with: Nicky, Israel, Sonny, and others. Things at home were never quite the same after that. I could feel the Lord pulling David more and more toward a full-time ministry among the gangs in New York. The members of our congregation in Philipsburg were understanding beyond belief, but it had become evident that David could not minister there *and* 350 miles away at the same time. His announcement to me was sudden but not unexpected.

"Gwen, honey, we're going to have to leave Philipsburg. I'm convinced that God wants me to go to New York on a full-time basis. We'll have to resign from the church and begin again on faith. I've no idea where He'll lead us but we've got to follow Him."

The Lord had prepared me for this moment. I knew He was calling us to other work. To my husband's infinite relief I replied calmly, "I know, David. I've heard His call too, and I've already said yes to Him."

Tearing Up Roots

Accepting the idea of moving away from Philipsburg was a great deal easier than doing it. For David, resigning from his pastorate meant leaving the flock of souls he had lovingly shepherded for five years. For me, it meant parting from my closest friends, moving out of the little parsonage we'd built and transformed into a home, and giving up the wonderful security of knowing what was expected of me. The work to which David was being called sounded challenging and exciting—but I wondered just where I would fit into his new career. What did the future hold for the children and me?

In the year or more between the Farmer trial and David's official resignation from the church, I had been introduced to some of the unusual people who were now a part of my husband's life. Occasionally he brought home to Philipsburg an assortment of young men—Nicky Cruz and Sonny Arguinzoni among them—to visit with us and to take part with him in various speaking engagements. Before bringing them to our home, David was careful to fill me in on their pasts so that I could appreciate the miracle of their new lives in Christ. Sometimes, however, his graphic descriptions did more to frighten me than to inspire me.

Nicky still teases me about what happened one time when he was our houseguest. David had a pastoral obligation that took him out for the evening, leaving Nicky alone with the children and me. I didn't think my nervousness showed, but when I retired early that evening I was careful to lock the bedroom door behind me. To a youngster like Nicky, the sound of that bolt sliding into place was an unmistakable symbol of mistrust. Fortunately, he had already passed that phase of his rehabilitation where he was most sensitive and defensive. He was now a mature enough Christian to wait patiently for me to gain confidence in him as I witnessed firsthand the work of Jesus in his life. Before long, Nicky had become one of my trusted friends.

Such contacts with the boys David brought home greatly increased my appreciation of the miraculous way the Lord was using him. But they also convinced me that I still had a great deal to learn.

The Lord must have known, however, that I wasn't yet ready for this higher education. Once David's resignation from the church became official, we had to make some quick decisions about our next move. When we finally found time to sit down together and discuss our immediate future, I realized that David had already given our situation a great deal of thought.

"One thing is sure," he began. "You and the kids can't sleep on a cot in the office the way I do when I'm in the city overnight—and I'm afraid we can't afford a separate apartment just now." After dropping that bit of information, David waited somewhat apprehensively for my reaction.

I understood why we couldn't live in his office on Staten Island's Victory Boulevard. It was almost too small for the office work being done there, and certainly could not house a family of five. In the back of my mind, however, I had cherished the hope that we could afford a small apartment of our own in New York.

"Well, we have to get settled somewhere before September," was all I could think of to say. "You aren't forgetting that Debbie begins first grade this fall, are you?"

"No, I'm not forgetting that, and I don't want to be moving her around during her first year in school. Let's face it, Gwen. The children all need a more stable environment than I can give them now in New York. With Gary so young and the girls needing room to play—"

David's voice trailed off, and his next words were a halting question. "Do you suppose your folks would mind if you and the kids stayed with them just for the school year, until we can afford a decent place in New York?"

I was *afraid* that was what David had in mind! Returning home to my parents was obviously the most sensible move we could make at this point, but I found the idea most unappealing. Mom and Dad would be willing to have us, I knew, and they had plenty of room. They were now living in my Grandmother Carosso's four-story house in Forest Hills. It was big enough to accommodate the five of us on the ground level, completely apart from my parents' quarters on the floor above. A private entrance and separate cooking facilities would make it possible for us to lead a life of our own.

Nevertheless, I could hardly bear the thought of being dependent on Mom and Dad after seven years of marriage and three children. Remembering my father's warnings against marrying a minister with no predictable income, I found it difficult to accept the idea of spending a year under his roof as a nonpaying guest. It took several days of earnest prayer and David's quiet encouragement before I could bring myself to agree to this humbling arrangement and write my parents for permission to move back home. The return mail brought a letter expressing their approval of our plans and their eagerness to help.

Before the summer was over, we had said our last tearful good-byes to the Philipsburg church. David took the children and me to Pittsburgh, then headed east to New York.

I will always be grateful to my parents for the kindness they showed us during our year in Forest Hills. Mom proved to be a non-interfering mother, who knew just when to offer help and when to back off. She made it easy for me to accept their assistance with genuine gratitude. Dad had mellowed to an amazing degree over the years since the grandchildren started arriving. He was so pleased to have Debbie, Bonnie and Gary close at hand that he never made reference to our circumstances or uttered anything like "I told you so." I was thankful for his tact and pleasantly surprised to discover how much I enjoyed being close to my family and old friends once again. I understood the folks who lived in this region and felt at home with their lifestyle. Much as I missed Philipsburg, I suspected that I would have missed it a great deal more if we had been living in New York. The adjustment to a totally new way of life still lay in the future. For now, just tearing up the deep roots that tied me to Philipsburg was difficult enough.

The hardest part, of course, was being separated from David. Although he had made many trips to New York during his last year in the pastorate and I had grown impatient at times with his inopportune absences, Philipsburg had at least been his acknowledged home. Now, however, his base of operations was clearly in New York. His speaking engagements took him all over the country, but the ministry itself was rooted in the urban ghettos. That was where his dreams and visions were taking form and where his life was centered. Forest Hills was just a place to visit.

David tried hard to spend part of every weekend with us, usually arriving late Saturday night. It was seldom that he could make it for the whole weekend and often he didn't make it at all. Short as they were, however, the weekends we spent together were times of great fellowship and joy for all of us. David often arrived weary from travel or from late nights spent ministering on the streets, but he never let his fatigue keep him from enjoying to the fullest his hours with his family. We attended church together, took long walks when the weather was good—sometimes carrying along a picnic lunch—shared in family prayer and worship, and enjoyed the luxury of extended conversation.

When David returned to the city on Monday morning, it took me a full day to become adjusted to his absence. Much as I missed him as a husband, I missed him most as the children's father. David was virtually losing a year in the lives of his children—a year that would never come again. Debbie at six was a happy-go-lucky child who never gave me any real trouble. With her blond curls and big brown eyes, she looked and acted much the way I had at that age, and she was easy to discipline. In her first year of school, she was growing up fast. She delighted in each new challenge and eagerly shared with me her excitement in learning to read and do arithmetic. As I listened to her happy chatter and watched her grow, I knew that David was missing far more than he realized.

Bonnie was another story. At four-and-a-half she was more active and more mischievous than Debbie had ever been. Her bouncing brown ringlets and flashing eyes proclaimed to the world that she was her daddy's child, heir to his boundless energy and enthusiasm. She had to test each rule or regulation for herself before deciding whether to obey it. To deal with her required more patience, firmness and wisdom than I possessed, and I noted ruefully that David made more headway with her in the few hours he was home on the weekends than I did all week long. This observation made me miss him all the more.

But it was Gary, changing rapidly from a lovable baby into the happiest of toddlers, who made me really long for David to share the daily joys and trials of parenthood. David, I knew, hated to miss these months with his family, but his mind was so fully occupied with his new work that he didn't feel the loss as keenly as I did.

Each weekend, David tried to bring us up to date on what was happening in New York. His ministry was moving so rapidly that I found it hard to keep up with events as they unfolded.

Shortly after the successful rallies at St. Nick's Arena, the ministry had acquired a board of directors and the name Teen-Age Evangelism. Under David's direction a small group of enthusiastic ministers and lay people, starting with many dreams and hopes but almost no financial resources, had put on a series of TV programs and distributed printed evangelistic materials to high school students. Meeting with only limited success by these methods, they were forced to conclude that street ministry, the one-to-one encounters David had first stumbled upon, and crusade rallies like the ones David had held at St. Nick's, were the most effective approaches to evangelistic work among young people in the ghettos. Now they were trying to round up support for a home where new converts could be taken for more complete rehabilitation. David was never more enthusiastic than when he was sharing his ideas for that home.

"We've got our eye on a place in Brooklyn," he told us one Sunday, "on Clinton Avenue. Boy, do we ever need it! Our rallies are drawing the kids in and the Spirit has been working miracles among them. I've never seen anything like the power of Jesus when He reaches out to touch these kids. But then so many of them get discouraged when they try to put their new faith into practice. They just can't get it together in their own homes; everything in their surroundings is working against them. If we can find the resources for that home, Gwen, we can give them a stable Christian environment and a chance to grow to maturity in Jesus."

As he shared his vision with me, I began to catch more and more of his excitement. My own prayer life found greater direction and purpose in supporting the efforts of this small group of Christians with their huge plans for bringing the love of Jesus to young people who had never known any real love before.

David's optimism about the future *was* contagious. "We've seen so many miracles already!" he'd exclaim. "The Lord has sent such wonderful people to help us—Stanley Berg, Paul Dilena, and Vincente Ortez. And it's incredible the way money seems to become available at just the right moment. Every time we think we've struck out, that there's just no way to do what we feel the Lord wants, a door opens somewhere and we are able to go ahead. I just *know* the Lord will provide that home for the kids at exactly the right time. Wait and see, Gwen. He's only begun this work. There's a lot more coming."

I believed him. There was no doubt in my mind that the Holy Spirit was engineering this entire fantastic ministry. David and the people who supported the work were useful instruments in the Lord's hands, but clearly the whole project was beyond human comprehension or manipulation. I watched it all from afar with growing wonder.

Wonder turned to disbelief when David came home and announced that a book was being written about the ministry.

"A book!" I stammered. "Isn't it too soon? I mean, you've only *begun* to get things rolling."

I was really taken aback at the thought that this struggling new work might be prematurely sprung on an unreceptive public. To make it the subject of a book seemed a bit presumptuous, and I told David so.

"No, honey. I don't think it's too early to *begin* to share God's plan with others. That's really what I'm doing when I travel around to all those meetings; I'm telling them what we are being called to do. Think of how many *more* people can be reached through a book. John and Elizabeth Sherrill are the ones we'll be working with on this project. John's with *Guideposts,* you know. I have a feeling that the Lord can really use this book. By the time it's completed, who knows how big a story it will tell?"

My own doubts began to diminish in the face of David's enthusiasm, and they vanished completely after John and Tib Sherrill entered our lives. Interviews, lengthy phone calls, and their impromptu visits for taping information soon became a way of life for us. All of this was such a departure from our normal quiet existence that I became more and more convinced that only the Lord could be responsible for what was happening. I often found myself asking Him just where it would all end.

All the activity, anticipation, and excitement made the months of separation seem far shorter than I had dared expect. Soon winter lost some of its bluster and warmer breezes were teasing us with thoughts of an early spring. At the end of an unusually balmy Thursday, David appeared unexpectedly at our door with a surprise invitation.

"How about driving to New York tomorrow?" he asked. "Paul and Sonia Dilena have been asking to meet you and the children, and they finally *ordered* me to come get you and bring you to their house for dinner tomorrow night. Do you think we could take Debbie out of school for one day?"

Nothing could have kept me from saying yes to such an invitation. I had heard so much about what great friends Paul and Sonia had been to David that I was eager to meet them. And I felt it was high time for me to be getting a look at the city that was to become home for our family. The children fully shared my enthusiasm, and we had no trouble getting them up the next morning and ready for the long drive to New York.

The Dilenas' home was in a section of Long Island called Sunnyside. When we pulled up to their address, I knew we were not in that part of New York where David had his ministry. The neighborhood was quietly elegant and the Dilenas' home looked to me like a palace. I tried hard not to seem awed by the tasteful furnishings and sophisticated decor. It was a comfort to discover that Paul and Sonia themselves were down-to-earth, sensible people. Their warm welcome soon put me at ease.

Paul, a captain in the New York Police Department, knew as much about the problems of the urban teenager as anyone in New York. David had been drawn to him both by his honesty in admitting the overwhelming dimensions of these problems and by his great faith in the Lord's ability to deal with the impossible. Sonia was as plainspoken as Paul, and she described to me in detail just what our husbands were dealing with in their work with the gangs.

"There are prostitutes and pushers and every hardened type of female you can think of out there on those streets," she told me frankly, "and the best thing you can do for David is to love him to death whenever you can. That's the best antidote in the world for the temptations that are going to be constantly before him."

That David might actually be susceptible to the wiles of some of the very girls he was trying to reach for the Lord was unthinkable to me, but Sonia's blunt warning served to jolt me out of my complacency. I never forgot her advice.

After a delicious dinner spiced by lively conversation, Paul pushed his chair back from the table and said to David, "What do you say we show Gwen the house on Clinton Avenue before you go home?"

David looked at me inquiringly and said, "It's up to Gwen. Do you want to see the *real* city, honey?"

Did I? My only concern was the children, who were tired from the long drive. Sonia quickly solved that problem. "I'll stay here with the children," she volunteered. "You really won't want them along with you this first time."

Minutes later, we left the warmth and security of the Dilenas' home and were walking down concrete steps into a yawning black hole in the sidewalk to board a subway for Brooklyn. The underground passage was a confusion of flashing lights, graffiti-decorated walls, and the roaring of passing subway cars. I clutched David and Paul tightly as we boarded a car and sped off into that seemingly endless gray tunnel toward Brooklyn.

By the time we emerged aboveground again, my sense of adventure had dimmed considerably. The tall buildings, crammed together so tightly, all seemed to have crumbling front steps and broken windows. In spite of the fact that the evening had become chilly, there were still crowds of people on the streets—some of them children no bigger than Bonnie. Everything seemed gray with dirt, raucous with traffic sounds, and rank with a mixture of assorted odors.

The Clinton Avenue building we had come to see— the house that David and the board of Teen-Age Evangelism were so eager to purchase—didn't appear to me significantly more promising than all the others around it. I found it hard to hide my disappointment.

How on earth does David do it? was my silent cry. *Dear Jesus, how can anyone come out here on these streets and minister your love to these people? How will I stand living in such a place?*

I had little to say on the return trip to Long Island, though I sensed that Paul and David were both waiting for my reaction. After picking up the children at the Dilenas' and thanking our hosts for their hospitality, David and I drove to Staten Island to spend the night with friends. As we drove through the city, with the children sound asleep on the back seat, I asked David the same question I had asked the Lord: "How will I ever learn to live in such an awful place? How can we possibly make our home and bring up our children here?"

David was prepared for my doubts. Reaching over to give my hand a reassuring squeeze, he replied calmly, "In the first place, Gwen, we won't be living on Clinton Avenue. I promise to find a place in a decent neighborhood before I bring you and the kids to New York. In the second place, you know the answer to your question as well as I do. You've said it yourself many times. No one but Jesus would even try to reach out to the kinds of people you saw tonight. He's the One who gives me the courage and He's got plenty more for you. Just let Him take care of things. Only the Lord can give us the strength to cope with problems like these."

The realization that I would soon have to put David's brave theory to the test made our remaining few months in Pittsburgh seem like a welcome reprieve. David's announcement, in midsummer, that he had rented an apartment for us on Victory Boulevard, brought me mixed emotions. I was thankful that our year of separation was ending, but at the same time I was very much aware that the real test of my faith was about to begin. As I packed our belongings once again, I prayed earnestly for Jesus' help and strength in the days ahead. I was sure that David was right, only the Lord could successfully transform me into a city-dweller.

City Living

I looked around the cluttered room and felt like crying. So this was our new home: four rooms on the first floor of an aging house in Staten Island. The packing boxes and furniture, standing around in complete disarray, made the apartment look terribly small and untidy. And the job of transforming it into a livable home seemed overwhelming.

A naked, burnt-out light bulb hung from its cord in the middle of the living room, looking as forlorn and useless as I felt. Our new quarters hadn't seemed quite so drab the day before, when David and I had moved the furniture and crates into the four empty rooms. This morning, however, David had gone off on another speaking trip. He hadn't even had time before leaving to run out and buy a light bulb to replace the one that was now the object of my annoyance.

I couldn't recall where David had gone this time. But I remembered well the rueful look on his face as he waited by the door that morning with suitcase in hand. After the girls had given him the usual big farewell display, with sticky kisses and warm hugs, he gathered Gary up in his arms before turning to me.

"Gwen, what can I say? I feel like a heel leaving you in all this mess—but I really can't help it. This trip just can't be postponed. I'll be home this weekend. Promise you won't try to do it all before I'm here to help, OK?"

My husband looked so downcast that I forced myself to rally and give him a reassuring smile before his departure.

"It's all right, Dave. Honest it is. We'll be fine. Things *are* in a mess now. But even if you were here I doubt if you'd spend your time cleaning out cabinets and washing woodwork. Just get along to your crusade and let the Lord use you. There'll be plenty left for you to do when you get back."

David's relieved grin and "Thanks, honey. You're great!" were reward enough at the moment for the effort I'd made to hide my dismay. Now, however, as I began to tackle the crates of dishes piled up in the kitchen, I found it hard to recover the attitude of cheerful competence I had displayed for my husband's sake.

As I washed plates and tried to find ways for the children to occupy themselves, I began to call on Jesus for His help in battling the emotions that threatened to overwhelm me. At first my prayer was a recital of complaints: "Lord Jesus, why must David *always* be away at the exact times when I need him the most? I don't mind the work, Lord—but this place is beyond help. How will I ever get used to living here? Where will the children play? And how can I get up enough courage to go out on those streets? Help me, Jesus! I'm scared to death!"

Jesus heard me out and then gently called me to repentance. Soon I found myself confessing that I was again allowing the old sins of anger and jealousy to take root in my life. I was angry that David was out in the limelight speaking to crowds of admirers while I was confined to this chaotic, rundown apartment with three small children nagging me for something to do. Instead of being thankful that our family could be together again, I was allowing self-pity, resentment and fear to dominate my thinking. Things had gotten so out of focus that I was even feeling hostile toward a worn-out old light bulb for refusing to give me illumination.

"I'm sorry, Jesus," I finally sobbed, my tears splashing into the dishwater. "I know that what's really wrong is here within me. Root out my resentment, anger and petty jealousy. Fill me again with your own loving Spirit, and give me your peace and your joy. Oh, Lord, teach me to be your person in this place!"

Jesus heard that prayer of confession, accepted my repentance, and answered my cry for help. As I stood there at the sink, there came flooding into my soul the reassurance that I was indeed in the place where God wanted me and that He would sustain me by the power of His Spirit. Along with that reassurance came renewed energy and patience with the children. By mid-afternoon, the Lord and I together had wrought a minor miracle by getting that apartment into reasonable order.

Then I had to call on Jesus for the courage to venture out on the streets in order to locate a store where I could buy a light bulb and other necessary supplies. Our up-stairs neighbors, who were also our landladies, were happy to supply me with directions to the nearest grocery store. These wonderful women—an elderly widow and her unmarried daughter—had learned from their pastor that David needed housing for his family. They responded by offering us a first-floor apartment in their home at a price far below the current rental rates. I was grateful to them for the kindness that enabled our family to be reunited, and was thankful to have trustworthy advisers to help orient me to this neighborhood.

Carefully following the directions I had written down, I set out on foot with Debbie, Bonnie, and Gary to travel the three blocks to the grocery store. By the time I had carried Gary and herded the girls across two busy inter-sections crammed with cars, buses, trucks, and taxis, I was almost too unnerved to make my purchases. The sidewalks were nearly as congested as the streets. Instinctively, the children and I pressed closer together to keep from getting separated in the throng of hurrying people.

The return trip, with the added burden of grocery bags, was even more hazardous than the first part of our expedition. When we finally reached our apartment and shut the door on the clamor in the street, those four rooms seemed like a haven of refuge. I breathed a prayer of thanksgiving for the Lord's protection and for the friendliness these walls suddenly seemed to offer. At the same time, I told Jesus frankly that it would take a true miracle for me to be able to venture out onto the city streets with

anything resembling confidence. Once again I felt His reassurance—perhaps tinged with just a trace of amusement.
By the time David returned on Saturday the apartment
was more than merely livable. It was actually beginning
to look like home. David declared that I had worked
wonders in the four days of his absence.

"I don't know how you did it, honey," he exclaimed
as he walked slowly from room to room, viewing the fruits
of my labors. "You've really transformed this place!"

As I basked in the warmth of my husband's admiration, I was glad that only Jesus and I knew that the greatest transformation—the most *necessary* transformation—
had been in me rather than in our apartment.

In a few weeks school began for Debbie and Bonnie.
David, when he wasn't traveling, spent his waking hours
either in Brooklyn or at the office on Victory Boulevard.
In the mornings, Gary and I were free to explore our
environs—and with familiarity came the confidence I
never thought I'd feel. I even began to enjoy our tours of
exploration. There was always something new to see or
to experience. At first I found it unsettling to encounter
so many people of different races. But soon I accepted
the rich diversity of color, ethnic background, and even
language as a stimulating rather than a frightening experience. For me and for the children, our immediate neighborhood provided an ongoing, broadening education in
humanity.

The biggest help in getting acclimated to city living
came from the church we joined within a few weeks after our move—the same church that had helped us find

our present home. I discovered that dedicated Christians are very much the same everywhere, whether part of a small rural parish or surrounded by urban sprawl. The members of our new church welcomed us with the same warmth, love, and helpfulness we had experienced in Philipsburg. People came forward to offer us transportation, baby-sitters, help in locating a doctor or a dentist. All the assistance a group of people *could* give was provided by that congregation when we began attending their church.

Soon the children were happily involved in Sunday school and Bible Club activities, and I ventured once more to join the choir. Whether David was home on Sunday or not, we were able to participate as a family in this warm fellowship of believers. The church began to fill for us the same central role it had for my family when I was growing up. And this close relationship with people who loved the Lord as we did made every other adjustment easier.

It was through the church that I met Bunny Olson—a pretty, vivacious, dark-haired girl who was Debbie's Sunday school teacher. I liked her immediately for her friendliness and her quick sense of humor. When we discovered that we were almost neighbors (she lived less than a mile away) and that we both had preschool children, we became fast friends. We made many shopping trips with little tykes in tow, shared lunches at each other's apartment, and took the children on cookouts, hikes, or outings to the zoo.

Everyone should have a friend like Bunny. She made

me laugh, she helped me discover the things that were fun to do in the city, and she shared her life of faith without self-consciousness. I thank God still for His kindness in providing a special friend in Staten Island just for me.

Once or twice I tried to assist David in the office when a large mailing was being prepared. It soon became obvious, however, that my "help" was less an asset than a liability. With Gary being such an active young man and Bonnie arriving home from kindergarten at noon, my contributions to my husband's ministry were limited by family responsibilities.

I did accompany David to some of the rallies he held in an unused theater on the East Side, when I could get a sitter or bring the children along. At such times I played the decrepit old organ to accompany the singing. I considered it a privilege to be even an occasional witness to the work God was doing with these young people, but I knew that my first priority was at home.

At first I found it hard to admit publicly that David's work was not mine as well. I knew where the Lord wanted me, but the expectations of others were sometimes hard for me to handle. Mom Wilkerson had come to the city following the death of David's dad and she was a visibly active participant in the youth work. When people met me for the first time they invariably asked, "And what do *you* do in the ministry, Gwen?" A real victory was won when I could finally answer those questions without launching into a lengthy and apologetic explanation. I learned to respond simply, "My work is at home, with the children."

Less than a year after our move, the home on Clinton Avenue became a reality. Teen-Age Evangelism was renamed Teen Challenge, and the Clinton Avenue house was called Teen Challenge Center. Now David had the additional responsibility of training and supervising the many new staff members who came to work at the center, most of them without salary. Through the rallies and the one-to-one witness of these consecrated young Christians, kids right off the streets were being miraculously touched by the powerful love of God. Just as David had predicted, many of those who had nowhere to go for nurture and growth came to the center for counseling. Some made the center their home until they became mature enough Christians to handle the overwhelming problems of their home environment.

Ministering to such confused young people as these—most of them alcoholics and heroin addicts—required an enormous amount of spiritual energy. David and his helpers needed to be upheld by the constant prayers of those who shared their concern and their awareness of the Lord's love and power. The children and I became regular prayer warriors on behalf of David and the entire Teen Challenge undertaking. From the time Gary was barely able to talk, he seemed to possess remarkable understanding about his father's work. He would pray long and hard to Jesus to help Daddy and to give him the strength he needed. We suspected then that we had a budding minister in the family.

David's personal commitment to this work was intense. I never have figured out how he found the time and energy to be so many places, doing so many different things. Not only did he conduct the rallies and oversee the running of the center, he also carried the burden for financing the entire operation. He traveled all over the country, placing the needs of Teen Challenge before any group of people who asked him to speak. From many diverse sources love offerings and gifts came pouring in— always enough to meet the immediate need, but never so much that any step or new direction could be taken with money in hand. Teen Challenge continued to be a ministry conceived in God's power and lived out by faith, one day at a time. I tried to live the same way.

During the brief intervals David was at home, I knew he needed rest and relaxation, not a whole batch of new problems to solve. That's when I began telling him only the good news of our family: the things we'd done for fun, the children's small achievements, and the indication of spiritual growth I had noted in their lives. David's gratitude for a home where order and tranquility prevailed was so rewarding that I determined to keep it that way for him. I felt personally responsible for shielding him from any troublesome matters, like the recurrent pains I'd been having in my right side. I barely mentioned this problem to David. And when I did, I emphasized the doctor's reassurance that it was probably just a swollen ovary—a common condition that would clear up spontaneously. David had enough on his mind without worrying about such a trivial complaint.

During the third year after our move to Staten Island, the Lord made available to us, through a miracle I've yet to comprehend, a lovely little house of our own. Located just two blocks from our apartment, it was not large but *was* new and convenient. Its most valuable feature was a small backyard, where our children could play safely with their friends.

With comfortable living quarters for our family and the Teen Challenge Center a reality, I began to feel that we "had it made." After nearly three years of preparation, the Sherrills' book finally made its appearance in bookstores across the country. There in black and white, for all to read, was the story of God's love reaching into the ghettos of New York through a country preacher. And that country preacher was my own husband! We didn't know at that time that *The Cross and the Switchblade* was destined to be a best-seller, but we did see it as another example of the Lord's hand at work on behalf of Teen Challenge.

Soon after publication of the book, a new office building was completed right next to the center on Clinton Avenue—another venture in faith that came to fruition at precisely the needed moment. An abundant supply of volunteers were coming to the city to help at the center, and Jesus continued to draw troubled teens to Himself through their street ministry.

Looking more relaxed and content than I'd seen him in years, David came home one summer day in 1963 and announced that we were taking the children for a long-overdue vacation in Forest Hills. As I joyfully packed our suitcases for the trip, I chuckled to think how far I personally had come since those suitcases were unpacked in our dingy little apartment just three years earlier. David's theory, expressed after my first visit to the city, had been put to the test and I found it to be valid: Only Jesus could have brought me so far so fast. Only He could have banished my fears and given me the confidence, flexibility, and strength I needed to make a home for us in the city.

My gratitude welled up and spilled over into a spontaneous prayer of thanksgiving and praise. Life was getting better and better. I could hardly wait to see what would happen next.

Little did I know that the next turn in the road would lead into another crisis—one that would test me personally in ways I never could have imagined.

The Fiery Furnace

CHAPTER SEVEN

Why has the pain gotten so much worse? I wondered. I'd had bad attacks like this before, but I'd usually been able to get some relief after resting for a while. This time the stabbing knife in my side was relentless. All the way to Pittsburgh I'd clench my teeth to keep from gasping with each breath I took. David commented on my unusual quietness, but I passed it off as fatigue from packing. When he suggested a nap, I gratefully closed my eyes. If I pretended to be sleeping, I wouldn't have to try to make conversation.

You are not going to ruin this vacation, Gwen Wilkerson, I told myself angrily. *David and the children really need this time together, and Mom and Dad shouldn't have to be worrying about you while their grandchildren are around.* But my pep talk had no effect on the pain, and I could not hide it indefinitely.

"Gwen, why didn't you *say* something?" was David's worried query when he finally came upon me doubled up with pain in the bedroom in my parents' home. "Is it that old ovarian thing again? What can I do to help?"

"Nothing, Dave. I'm sure it will go away soon. It always does." I tried to divert his attention. But neither my husband nor my mother would buy my attempts at reassurance while I remained so obviously uncomfortable.

"David Wilkerson, you get that girl to the doctor," Mom ordered, having decided that some interference was justified at this point. "There's got to be something wrong if she's in that much pain." Grateful for Mom's backing, David called a local family practitioner who told him to bring me right over to see him.

The doctor's expression was grave when he finished his examination. After I dressed, he had David and me come into his office while he shared the reason for his concern. He had found a mass in the left side of my abdomen, and he didn't think it was the ovary. Further tests were needed to determine just *what* it was—the sooner the better.

"You'd better check in with a specialist when you get back to Staten Island," he advised. "And don't take your time doing it, either. I don't like the amount of discomfort you're having, and I don't like abdominal masses we can't explain."

Since the vacation was virtually ruined for everyone and was a total failure for me, we decided to return home the next day. Within a week I reported to the specialist who had been recommended to us, and suffered the discomforts and indignities of another examination, followed by abdominal x-rays.

When the doctor called a day or so later to ask how he could reach David at work, I was sure the news was bad.

Back in the specialist's office that afternoon, David and I held hands tightly while the doctor explained that the x-rays had confirmed the existence of a mass in my abdomen. It was *not* the ovary, and it had to come out right away.

"I don't want to alarm you unnecessarily," he concluded, "but we don't see many benign growths in that region and we simply cannot delay surgery. How soon can you be ready for admission to the hospital? By tomorrow? Wednesday?"

I couldn't believe he meant *that* soon! David was due to go out of town again on Wednesday. It was an important trip and I didn't want him to miss it. But who could stay with the children? And how could I bear to go into the operating room without the reassuring presence of my husband?

The word "colostomy" broke into my whirling thoughts and brought my mind back to what the doctor was saying. I wasn't sure what the word meant, but I didn't like the sound of it. When he went on to explain that a colostomy is a permanent bowel opening on the abdomen and that such a procedure would probably be necessary in my case, I liked it even less. The thought was so frightening that I couldn't bring myself to ask any questions about it or to discuss it with David after we left the office.

As David and I talked it over, we were both very much aware of the doctor's warning against delay. The urgency he displayed had shaken us both. Finally we agreed that we should call my parents and ask them to come the next day and stay with the children. I would enter the hospital on Wednesday and have the further studies that were needed on Thursday. David could make his trip and be back before the operation on Friday.

Making the necessary arrangements, explaining as much as I could to the children, and putting my house in order kept me so busy the next day that I had little time to think about what was coming. It was hard to convince myself that this was really happening to me, who had always been so healthy. True, I had been experiencing waves of fatigue lately and I'd lost some weight, but neither of these symptoms seemed surprising in view of the busy life I led. And I *felt* well—except for that pain. Women 32 years old don't get cancer, I told myself. Or do they?

David and I were careful to avoid the words "cancer" and "colostomy" as we talked and prayed together, but I was acutely aware of his concern. Several times I caught him staring at me with a worried, pained expression that fed my own growing anxiety. Each of us, however, was determined to put on a brave front for the other and for our family—an effort which deprived us of the opportunity to deal openly and honestly with the tears that were welling up within each of us.

By the time David left me at the hospital on Wednesday morning, I was wearied beyond belief from the effort of pretending I was not upset about what lay ahead. As soon as I was alone, I began to cry out to Jesus.

He heard my cry and responded to my need for the assurance of His presence and His love. As I read my

Bible in the intervals between the various tests and studies that were being performed on my passive, weary body, I found myself particularly drawn to the Old Testament account of the three Jewish exiles in Babylon whose faith was tried in a *literal* fiery furnace. I sensed the Lord speaking to me in that story from the book of Daniel. He seemed to be telling me that just as Shadrach, Meshach and Abednego had emerged unscathed from the fire, I would pass through the test before me without suffering permanent harm.

Suddenly I didn't have to *pretend* to be brave. By the time David returned from his trip Thursday night, I was able to greet him with a cheerful optimism that was based on God's word to me—not on a desire to hide my real feelings. When we prayed together this time, we were open and honest with each other and with God. During our prayer, David received the same sense of assurance that Jesus had already given me. When I was wheeled away to the operating room the next morning, we parted with the confidence that I was in the loving hands of the Great Physician.

My husband needed that confidence during the next five hours, for the surgery took longer than the doctor had anticipated. When I finally awoke back in my room, David's face was pale and drawn as he tried to reassure me.

"Gwen, you're going to be fine. They got it all, and you're OK now. Isn't that great news, honey? You'll be well in no time!"

I sensed more hope than assurance in David's voice,

but I was too weak and groggy to question him. I would find out the details later. Just now I only wanted to sleep. Mustering a faint smile, I murmured, "That's nice, Dave. We'll see about it; we'll see." Then I drifted back into a drug-induced slumber, where I could forget the pain in my side and postpone my return to harsh reality.

Later, of course, I had to be told the whole truth. The mass in my colon *had* been malignant and quite large. However, the surgeon had apparently succeeded in removing it all, along with some muscle tissue and a good deal of my intestine. To my great relief, a colostomy had not been necessary.

I thanked God that my body was left relatively intact, at least to all outward appearances. I thanked Him too that radiation therapy was not recommended at this time. Jesus had fulfilled His promise to bring me through this fiery trial, and I was willing to live one day at a time, knowing that the future was under His control.

My recovery amazed everyone, including me. The cancer within me had been draining my vitality for so long that its removal seemed to give me a new life. Within a few days after the surgery, I was walking around the halls of the hospital, handing out copies of *The Cross and the Switchblade* to everyone I met. When doctors and nurses expressed surprise at my rapid recovery, I witnessed eagerly to the miraculous power of the Lord and shared His promise of working all things together for good to those who love Him.

I was expected to spend 10 to 14 more days in the hospital after surgery. Instead, I went home at the end of a week, rejoicing in a new sense of well-being and praising God for sparing my life. More than ever, I felt that Jesus was watching over me.

David was watching over me too, and I was secretly pleased by his solicitude and even by his gentle scolding. Perplexed and slightly hurt by my decision not to trouble him with "little problems" like a developing cancer, he ordered me to rest more and to stop being a "reverse hypochondriac."

"Getting sick is nothing to be ashamed of, Gwen. What you should be ashamed of is not letting me know about it so that I could help you."

"I know, Dave," I replied meekly. "But I really hate to bother you when you have so much on your mind. I didn't know it was serious. I thought I could take care of myself without worrying you needlessly."

"Well, let's not have that kind of reasoning again, young lady. If you sense *anything* out of the ordinary going on, I want to know about it right away. Promise me, honey, that you'll be truthful and tell me if something isn't right. I don't want you to carry such a burden alone."

Even though David's continuing concern about my health gave me a warm feeling of being cherished, it also confirmed my suspicion that he and the doctors were not totally sure that all the errant cells had been removed from my body. However, I refused to let this suspicion destroy my peace of mind or my belief that God had healed me. I continued to live one day at a time and to gain strength and vitality daily.

The renewed pleasure I found in my children made

me realize how irritable I'd been with them in the last few months. David was right; I must never again try to hide from him anything pertaining to my health. I didn't plan to become a chronic complainer, but I did resolve to let my husband, as well as my doctor, know about any symptom that might crop up in the future.

That resolve was tested all too soon. I had been home just a little more than six weeks when I discovered a lump in my groin. I was sorely tempted to pretend it wasn't there. I was feeling great, and the lump wasn't painful. It couldn't be more cancer! But I had made a promise to David and I had to tell him about my discovery. He took me to my surgeon the very next day and neither of them tried to hide the facts from me this time.

"If you've got a lump *anywhere*, we have to assume it's a metastasis from the first tumor," the doctor told me. "We can't wait to see if it will go away. You must have *surgery—now!*"

Within two months after my first operation, I found myself back in the hospital, facing another trip to the operating room. Discouragement and fear had dropped on me like a heavy blanket, and all my assurance that the Lord would spare my life had evaporated. Fortunately, David's faith was a great deal stronger than mine as we sat together the night before the operation and prayed for a favorable report the next day.

"Dave, how many of these operations will I have to face? How often will I have this fear grab hold of me and rob me of all the joy of living? I can't stand the thought of having to examine myself every day for more lumps, more cancers." The desperation in my voice surprised even me.

As I watched David searching for some words of reassurance to give me, I had a guilty awareness that my negative attitude was adding to the heavy burden he himself was carrying. Already he'd been hurt by questions he was getting from fellow workers concerning our faith for healing. "Why is it that you are trusting God to heal the drug addicts, but you and Gwen are looking for her healing in surgery?" was the gist of the questioning.

David had tried to explain our viewpoint. While we know that Jesus is the source of all wholeness, all health, we believe that He often uses the knowledge, wisdom, and skill He has given His allies in the medical profession as His channel for healing—and we were convinced that in my case He wanted us to do exactly what the doctors recommended. Right now I would welcome the healing touch of God in *whatever* way He wanted to give it to me. Yet I was so afraid He had other plans.

"Gwen, honey," David's voice brought my wandering thoughts back to him again, "your faith that Jesus was going to deliver you from the fiery trial of your first operation helped me find the faith to believe that too. This time the situation seems to be reversed. I still believe He intends to bring you out of this whole and restored. This is just a test to see how much we are willing to trust Him. I just know it will turn out OK, honey, and I am willing to rest on the same promise He gave you last time."

We soon had confirmation that David's faith was justified. The lump turned out to be a benign fibrous tumor and removing it was a simple matter. In four days I was back home again and well on my way to normal good health.

I felt ashamed of myself for having doubted, even briefly, that Jesus would remain faithful. Although my medical status was unchanged by this minor operation, it had served to teach me a valuable lesson in trust. I felt certain that if there was a "next time," another lump somewhere in my body, I would be better prepared to cope with it. I might be a slow learner, but I would not soon forget the Lord's faithfulness to me in this time of trial.

As I convalesced from this second operation, I was touched by David's efforts to spend more time with me and the children. Sometimes I felt guilty for allowing him to give us such a high priority. Book sales for *The Cross and the Switchblade* were soaring by now, and there was talk of a movie. As a result of the book's popularity, David was receiving requests from all over the country to hold crusades and to meet with individuals interested in starting Teen Challenge centers in their cities. I knew how hard it was for him to take any time away from his work, and the fact that his nights and weekends at home had become more frequent rather than *less* frequent showed me how important his wife and family were to him. I concluded that I had definitely married the right man.

Once again the peace of the Lord reigned supreme in our lives. We had emerged from our personal fiery furnace with renewed faith in the power and love of God, and with a sense of having been delivered from the sin of taking life too much for granted. We had a deeper appreciation and love for each other, and we cherished our children with a tenderness that can be experienced only by those who have stared death in the face.

The whole world seemed touched by God's grace in the fall of 1963. Everywhere we looked, we saw signs of the Lord at work in the autumn colors of the occasional tree in our neighborhood, in the young lives being transformed at the Teen Challenge Center, and in the obvious healing of my own body. So great was my sense of well-being, of wholeness and rejuvenation, that I became convinced the Lord was behind the desire which had become increasingly insistent ever since my convalescence began. I was just waiting for the right moment to discuss it with David.

Another Miracle, Another Trial

CHAPTER EIGHT

🌹

"Gwen, that's crazy!" David's exclamation was close to a shout. He stopped dead in his tracks and stared at me as though I'd suddenly taken leave of my senses.

It was the exact response I'd been expecting and I was already prepared to defend my suggestion. For an opener, I smiled sweetly at him and replied, "No, it's not."

We were taking a stroll around the neighborhood—a favorite pastime during my convalescence and by now a firmly established routine whenever David was home in the evening. The sun had not quite disappeared behind the tall apartment buildings, but the air was becoming quite chilly when I had finally found the courage to blurt out the words that had just jolted my husband: "Dave, I want another child. I want us to have a baby."

"Now, honey," David began again, in the soothing tone one might use with an unreasonable child.

Quickly I interrupted him, launching into my carefully rehearsed arguments: "Don't tell me I've been through too much and that my health can't take it. I've never felt better in my life than I have this last month. I really believe that Jesus is behind this desire. I just *know* that a baby is part of His plan for us now."

By this time David had doubtlessly mustered a whole list of counter-arguments. I watched him swallow hard a few times, as if choking back the words.

"I don't know, Gwen. It just doesn't seem like a good idea. Yes, I *am* concerned about your health—but if you think the Lord is leading—"

His voice trailed off, and a thoughtful pause followed. Sensing that I had him on the defensive, I followed up my advantage. "I do, Dave. I really do think this idea came from Him."

A long silence settled over us then, as we walked slowly back to the house. Before we entered it, David put his arms around me and said, "Just promise me you'll talk to the doctor first. If he says it's OK—well, I'm willing to trust the Lord for the final answer."

I could hardly wait to call my doctor for an appointment. In his office, he listened soberly as I told him what I had in mind. His reply was not encouraging.

"Gwen, I know you're feeling great right now. You've made a remarkable recovery from very serious, very extensive surgery, and you feel relieved and grateful. But pregnancy would put added burdens on your body, *if* you can even conceive now—which I rather doubt."

He went on to explain how the surgery had so altered the muscles and supporting structures in my abdomen that conception would be highly unlikely, and the chance of carrying a baby to term greatly reduced. I barely heard him. If I was correct in believing that the idea of having another child had come from Jesus, all this technical discussion was really not important. Nevertheless, I had promised David I would ask, and I heard myself pose the question: "But would it be dangerous for me to *try?*"

"Dangerous?" he repeated. "No, I wouldn't say dangerous. Foolish perhaps—but not really dangerous."

By Christmas I knew I was pregnant. Jesus had granted me my heart's desire. How could I doubt that He would see me safely through to the successful delivery of a healthy child? The discomforts of pregnancy seemed a minor price to pay for the miracle baby the Lord was giving us.

During my pregnancy the pace of David's activities accelerated. His travels kept him crisscrossing the country—from California to Alabama to Michigan to New York. Within New York State, his speaking trips were aimed primarily at ensuring continued financial support for the Teen Challenge Center in Brooklyn. Outside New York, however, David was preaching the broad and simple message of salvation for all mankind in Jesus Christ. More and more, he was being called upon to minister to a diverse population of young people, most of them very different from those he worked with at the center. These were just ordinary kids who were hungry for God. They had never robbed a store or taken drugs or dropped out of society. David called them the "goodniks."

"Gwen, they *all* need Jesus," was his conclusion. "Maybe I'm not supposed to stay zeroed in on just the problem kids. I've met so many beautiful young people who are managing to survive in the present system, but who desperately want to get it all together so that they can make sense out of life. Only the Lord can do that for them."

I was struck by the thought that David's ministry might be coming full circle. He had started out as a traveling evangelist, and his first priority had always been to bring the love of Jesus into the lives of young people. Now I watched him hit the road again with a similar mission— only now the road stretched clear across the country and his ministry seemed to be to a whole nation of needy youngsters. He was even receiving requests to speak overseas. My country preacher was on the verge of becoming a world traveler. Already he was something of a celebrity. I was very proud of him, and proud to be carrying his child.

The baby was due to arrive in mid-July, but as I recalled how long Debbie and Gary had delayed their appearance, I decided not to expect anything to happen before August. Nevertheless, David felt uneasy about being out of town once the calendar read *July*, and he took the precaution of asking my mother to come and stay with me until after the baby's birth.

Surprisingly, my labor began right on schedule. Mom was there to stay with the children, and David—wonder of wonders—was in town and could actually take me to the hospital. This delivery was going to be a cinch. Seldom had every detail worked out so well.

My complacency was soon shattered. I was in labor for hours, with no apparent progress. David paced and prayed, and I fussed and fumed, all to no avail. Our miracle baby was proving to be downright uncooperative. With each labor pain my fatigue was growing.

After 18 hours of fruitless labor, the obstetrician checked my condition one more time, then turned to David and said, "Mr. Wilkerson, I think we had better go ahead and deliver the baby by Caesarean." David gave his consent without hesitation. He was willing to agree to anything that would bring this labor to an end, and so was I.

Minutes later I was being rolled down the hall on a stretcher, watching the ceiling lights flicker past and wondering just exactly what a Caesarean section entailed. I had been rather heavily sedated during the many hours of labor and my mind had not quite grasped the doctor's explanation. Not until I was on the table, draped with green sheets and locally anesthetized, did I realize that I was about to have another operation.

"Oh, Lord," I sighed, "I'm going to look like a battle victim by the time they are through cutting on me." But before I could voice my protest, I heard a reassuring cry and found myself gazing into the enraged face of my miracle baby. I couldn't believe it could happen that fast after all those hours of labor. But there he was, a ten-pound, five-ounce baby boy, with dark ringlets like Bonnie's and a round, chubby face like Gary's.

"He's just beautiful," I kept repeating again and again until I was fast asleep. The labor had taken its toll and I continued to find it hard to stay awake in the days that followed.

As David observed my fatigue and talked to my doctor, he concluded that I was going to need more help at home this time. Mom could not stay indefinitely, and Debbie—even though she was now a very competent 11-year-old—could not be expected to take care of the entire household *and* me. We needed full-time help, at least temporarily. David began to pray about it and to make inquiries.

A minister friend from Minnesota was the one who told us about Sondra. She was a member of his church, a lovely girl from a good Christian home. At 19, she was eager to leave her parents' farm and do something else with her life. On his friend's recommendation, David brought Sondra to Staten Island to relieve my mother. Within two weeks' time, our family had expanded to include two new members: Gregory Allen Wilkerson and Sondra Schaefer.

Sondra's remarkable efficiency and cooperation were most welcome. In spite of my delight at having a new son, I found it hard to get back on my feet again. My persistent fatigue and weakness were both discouraging and annoying. Sondra was the best helper I could ask for, but *I* wanted to take charge of my baby and be a full-time mother to Debbie, Bonnie, and Gary.

Often my impatience with the slowness of my recovery led me to do too much. The results were always the same. After working too hard and being on my feet too long at a time, I'd be back in bed for a couple of days, completely exhausted. Soon my prayers contained only one plea: "Lord, make me strong again for my family's sake."

The better part of a year passed before my body finally

began to respond to the enforced rest and pampering. By spring I was able to assume the full supervision of my children and to lend Sondra a hand with the housework.

During the months of my recuperation David had made a trip to Europe and many trips to California, where crusades and rallies were being held on behalf of new Teen Challenge ministries that were arising. I noticed that he grew less and less enthusiastic about his trips by air, but I had not yet suspected that he was beginning a battle of his own. It seemed that we were still sheltering each other from our own personal problems.

David was home for a fairly long stay when I began to suggest that we could no longer justify having full-time help. "I'm really almost as strong as ever now, David," I told him. "And it isn't fair to Sondra to keep her here when she isn't needed. Besides, the children are beginning to resent having so many bosses."

But David had ideas of his own. "Nope. We're going to give you help as long as *I* think you need it. I'd do it myself if I could be here all the time, but since I can't, I want to keep Sondra and I want you to let her help. You still get awfully tired, and four children are a lot to keep up with."

Within a few months, I was glad David had stuck to his guns. We made a decision to move to a larger home in Massapequa Park, Long Island, not far from Sonia and Paul Dilena. Staten Island was becoming increasingly congested, and our expanded family really needed more space than the three tiny bedrooms our little house afforded. Without Sondra's willing hands and youthful energy, the move would certainly have drained what little strength I had in reserve.

The new house was a split-level dream, with four bedrooms and a large fenced-in backyard. It was everything I could have wanted in a home, even before David unveiled his plans for adding a master bedroom suite on the third level.

With Sondra's help, our family settled quickly into the accommodating spaciousness of this lovely home. Two weeks after our move, we celebrated Greg's first birthday in our big backyard. I was a little tired, and I did miss Bunny and the church that had meant so much to us, but I was still as happy as I could ever remember being. Summer of 1965 was apparently *my* season.

David seemed determined to spoil me with both material comforts and personal attention. Not long after our move, he asked me to accompany him on a short speaking trip to Memphis. It had been years since I'd been able to travel with him, and I was delighted at the opportunity. Since Sondra was still there to stay with the children, we didn't need to call on my family for help this time, even though Mom and Dad now lived close by. They too had moved to Long Island following Dad's retirement.

When we boarded the plane for Memphis, I felt almost like a bride again. I was looking forward to this trip as a sort of second honeymoon.

Some honeymoon! I spent most of it in a strange hospital. We had barely gotten off the plane when I felt overwhelmed with tiredness—not the usual weariness from travel, but a weak feeling that was just suddenly there full-blown and threatened to knock me off my feet. A short time later at the hospital, I began to hemorrhage.

In spite of my fervent prayers that the Lord would stop the bleeding and make it possible for us to enjoy this long-anticipated vacation, the loss of blood became so alarming that I finally had to tell David what was happening. In very short order he had me admitted to a large general hospital just a few blocks from the hotel, and there I stayed until we boarded a flight for home two days later.

The doctors in Memphis confused us with their complicated jargon, but we were somewhat reassured by their statement that this episode was probably not related to the cancer that had been removed just two years earlier. I was not reassured, however, by their recommendation that I consider a hysterectomy.

David and I talked about this all the way home, and soon reached an impasse. All I could say was, "I don't want any more operations!" David's reply was always, "If it's *necessary,* you'll have to have one, Gwen."

The fact was that neither of us knew enough about my condition to make a responsible decision.

We needed good medical counsel, but at the moment we did not have a doctor. The surgeon who had performed the first operation was no longer in Staten Island, and we had not been living in Long Island long enough to establish any contacts with the medical community there.

David finally hit upon a plan. "Let's fly out to Michigan to see Dr. Berghuis. I'd trust his judgment any time, and it'll be reassuring to talk to a man who knows the Lord as well as medicine."

It was truly an inspired idea. Dr. John Berghuis was a longtime friend and supporter of David. He had been in New York many times for meetings on behalf of Teen Challenge, but he lived and practiced surgery in Adrian, Michigan. David's volunteering to fly there to consult him was evidence of my husband's high regard for his opinion. By now, David avoided planes whenever he could. The transatlantic flight the year before had greatly increased his long-standing aversion to air travel.

Nevertheless, after making a hasty call to our friend and receiving his invitation to come out at once to see him, we boarded yet another plane to see what a Christian doctor would have to say about my condition.

Essentially, Dr. Berghuis agreed with the doctors in Memphis. He strongly recommended a hysterectomy and doubted that my problem was related to the earlier surgery or to the cancer. "More likely this is a result of childbirth, the Caesarean, and just the wear and tear of being a woman," he told us. "But I would like to take a good look around when we do the hysterectomy, to make sure nothing else is wrong."

That settled it for David, and I had no choice but to give my reluctant consent to another operation. However, I made a mental resolution right then and there: "This is *it* for me and operations. I've had it with hospitals, surgery, and lengthy recuperation. I will *not* go through all of this another time."

I'm not sure what I thought I was accomplishing in

taking such a stand, but at this time both my body and my mind had reached their limit of tolerance. The hysterectomy would be my fourth surgical procedure in barely two years, and this was my fifth hospitalization. I was just plain tired.

My weariness was a much more serious factor than any of us realized at the time. The hysterectomy, skillfully performed by Dr. Berghuis, presented no problem, and his meticulous examination while I was under anesthesia reassured us all that my earlier surgery had been entirely successful. But I had no reserve whatsoever for the new period of convalescence which awaited me. Perhaps this is why I soon found myself going through the blackest period of my life.

A Personal Prison

❦

Dr. Berghuis tried to warn us. David was his houseguest for the two weeks I remained in the hospital recuperating from the operation. During that time our friend discussed with us in detail what to expect after the procedure I'd just been through. He talked to us together, he chatted with each of us privately, and it was obvious that he spoke out of considerable experience and wisdom. As we later learned to our sorrow, his message also contained a great deal of the prophetic.

"You've been through quite an ordeal these past couple of years, Gwen," he reminded me (quite unnecessarily). "I'm sure you know about allowing time to recover your physical strength. You cannot push nature's healing process. That's God's own timing, you know."

I *did* know. The periods required for recuperation from my last three operations had varied widely. I'd found the healing process especially slow after Greggy's delivery by Caesarean. I assured Dr. Berghuis that I could be patient this time.

"What I'm afraid you *aren't* prepared for," he replied,

"is the emotional stress this particular operation might produce. Much of it can be explained by physiology—hormone changes and all of that. Most women don't realize what a profound effect a total hysterectomy can have on their emotional equilibrium."

It didn't make sense to me. Why should I expect any more emotional turmoil after *this* operation than I had after the others? But Dr. Berghuis had more to say, and I tried hard to understand what he was telling me.

"You see, Gwen, while many women experience only minimal adjustment difficulties after a hysterectomy, *some* women—especially those who are relatively young like yourself—suddenly feel useless. They seem to think that the loss of their childbearing ability has stripped them of any purpose in the scheme of things. Others feel that their husbands don't love them anymore that they've lost their attractiveness and their ability to hold their husbands' affections. Many women report overwhelming feelings of loneliness, depression, jealousy, and self-hatred."

Dr. Berghuis had my full attention now. His expression was so solemn that I felt some apprehension stirring within. Noting my concern, he spoke to me in a gentler tone.

"I'm telling you all of this, Gwen, because I want you to be prepared to do battle in the months ahead. I'm convinced you are physically sound now. But I'm just as convinced that you will have *some* struggle with your emotions before you are back to normal again. After all, you've been through four operations in two years, and that leaves you even more vulnerable to the aftereffects of a hysterectomy."

Satisfied that he had given me fair warning, Dr. Berghuis smiled warmly and gave my shoulder a comforting pat. "Just remember that you are a charming, worthwhile woman with a husband who loves you and four children who need you. Above all, remember that Jesus has you in His care. Lean on Him heavily when things get rough. He's the only One who can make this transitional period shorter and easier."

I appreciated our friend's concern, but I was fairly certain that his warning was unnecessary in my case. Having survived the prolonged period of recuperation that followed Greggy's birth, I was sure I could cope with anything that came along this time. I had good help at home, and David had already demonstrated his devotion by staying with me the whole time I was in Michigan. No, I wasn't like the women he described. If there was anything I had learned in the 13 years of our marriage, it was how to handle those very emotions Dr. Berghuis was talking about. I was weak from this last operation, but I'd find the way back with the Lord's help. I knew all about *His* faithfulness too.

During the flight home, David and I discussed Dr. Berghuis' advice. We both appreciated his desire to help us avoid the possible pitfalls, but we tended to minimize his concern. David's remark pretty well summarized my own feelings, "I guess he's seen so many folks who haven't learned to trust Jesus in such situations that he feels he has to give that warning to everyone. But surely if anybody can cope with stress, *we* can."

We then smiled at each other as we remembered the times of adjustment we'd been through. The rest of the way home we held hands and reminisced about earlier days.

After our plane landed at Kennedy Airport, we put the warnings out of our minds altogether and simply rejoiced in the successful surgery, our happy homecoming, and all the blessings our Lord had given us. It was good to be back with the children and they seemed very glad to see us. Debbie, who was turning 12 that fall, had begun to chafe under the authority of a "governess," as she insisted on calling Sondra. She felt that she and Bonnie were now old enough to help with the housework and the care of Gary and Greg. It was clear that she hoped my return home would mean Sondra's early departure.

Sondra was her usual sweet self and pretended not to notice the girls' growing coolness toward her. I myself felt sure that we would soon outgrow our need for her help, but at the moment I was glad she was still around. Such reliable assistance was hard to find, and I was still too weak to assume full responsibility for the housework and the care of two active boys—seven-year-old Gary and one-year-old Greggy.

We had barely gotten home and established something of a family life once again when David's work began to pick up steam and make great inroads into his time with us. Calls from around the country and around the world came into the Teen Challenge Center as *The Cross and the Switchblade* reached an ever-widening audience. Don

Murray was consulting with David about a film version of the book, and Pat Boone was interested in playing the role of David.

As I watched all this taking place, I realized that David was becoming a real celebrity—a public figure. It was then that the first stirrings of malcontent arose in my private thoughts. Even though I knew David was not being led by a desire for personal recognition, I began to wonder how all of this attention would affect him. He had *begun* his work under the leadership of the Spirit of God, but could any man remain unaffected by all this attention? So I began to watch David for signs of an inflated ego. I was ashamed of my thoughts and knew I wasn't being fair to my husband. There had been no change in him; he was still walking in the Lord's way. Still, I could not turn off the suspicions and fears that persistently buzzed around in my mind.

As David's travels increased, so did my impatience with the slow rate of my recovery. My energy level remained at low ebb and I sometimes felt that I would *never* be normal again. Being left at home while David traveled bothered me now as never before. I wanted to see the places where he was ministering and meet the people who were becoming his friends. I wondered sometimes if they even knew he *had* a wife. Just now, however, it was clearly out of the question for me to travel with him. I still became overwhelmingly fatigued with the least effort around the house.

Before long my frustrations were being transferred to Sondra and the children. I became picky about the appearance of our home and snapped at Sondra if she didn't do things just the way I would do them, or organize the work as efficiently as I thought I could. If the children left a toy out of place or walked into the house with dirty hands or feet, I gave them a harangue about the impossibility of keeping a decent home with no cooperation from them.

Sondra was wise enough to accept my criticism without comment, and even the children tolerated my outbursts with remarkably little resentment. I knew I was behaving badly, however, and my shame contributed to a growing feeling of guilt. Dr. Berghuis' warnings about moodiness and irritability began to make sense to me now. It was some comfort to know that this was not an unexpected reaction. But I still berated myself for my lack of self-control.

"Jesus, help me!" became my constant cry in those early days at home. I wanted to say more. I longed to talk with Him about my thoughts and fears, and to draw from His abundant supply the love and strength I needed to cope with the emotions that were threatening to overwhelm me. But prayer had suddenly become difficult and my devotional life hard to sustain. Although my need for the Lord was greater now than ever before, the time I was spending in fellowship with Him began to dwindle. This bothered me considerably at first, but gradually it seemed less and less important.

What *was* important to me was to keep myself from falling apart over every little disappointment or normal frustration of living. The children's small disagreements became major battles in my mind, and I could not stand to hear them tease one another. When Debbie and Bonnie tested Sondra's authority to direct them in some way, I could not or would not back her up. I just became upset and tense and sniped at all three of them with an ever-sharpening tongue.

My sarcasm and bitter words surprised everyone who heard them. They especially surprised me. *That's not you, Gwen,* I'd scold myself. *You've never talked like that in your life.* Then I'd go have another good cry and try harder than ever to stay in control.

At first David was spared most of this turmoil. He was away so much that he didn't see the worst of my outbursts, and Sondra and the children were too loyal to tell tales to him about me. When David was home, I knocked myself out trying to play the role of a good mother and loving wife.

To tell the truth, I was desperately afraid of what might happen if my husband knew what I was really like on the inside. After all, I reasoned, I wasn't much good for anything any more. I had developed a habit of falling apart a couple of times a year and requiring a major repair job. What kind of man would put up with a wife like that for very long? If David knew how badly I was coping now, he'd probably give up on me completely. Sonia's warning about the temptations my husband would be facing in his work kept echoing in my mind. David was now working with all kinds of young people. How could I hope to compete if I let him know what a shrew I was becoming?

Such reasoning led me to spend a lot of time on my appearance and to hide from David, as best I could, the desperation I felt. I *had* to. It seemed to me that my very life depended upon it.

By continuing this charade, I succeeded only in keeping my husband at a distance at the very time I needed his help and genuine understanding more than ever. The effort of putting on an act took more from me than I realized, and my tension soon became apparent even to David.

When David was home, he tried to bring me into his own devotional times in an effort to help me find the needed strength in the Lord. These attempts failing, he prayed *for* me and spent long hours holding me up to Jesus for His help. He also counseled Sondra in her predicament and tried to give the children some understanding of the situation. He made a superhuman effort to be available to all of us as much as possible. The problem centered on me, however, and I was beyond the reach of human help.

Throughout the whole ordeal I maintained our family's routines and public image to the best of my ability.

I continued to play an active role in the church. Perceptive observers may have noticed that I seemed a little tired and distant, but I was still "among those present," at least in body. My spirit, imprisoned by fear, guilt, resentment and suspicion, was far from the Lord, and I felt like a hypocrite just going through the motions of being a Christian. I was sure that if all those good church people knew what I was like on the inside, they would put me out of their fellowship for good.

My fear that someone *would* find out what was going on inside me made me keep everybody at arm's length. My own mother lived a few blocks away, and I had friends like Bunny and Sonia who would gladly have dropped everything to be of help to me, but I didn't dare draw them into my confidence. I'm sure I fooled no one. Mom in particular knew me too well not to recognize that I was putting on an act. But since she was not the kind to offer unsought advice or to "drop in" uninvited, I could easily keep her at a distance. She, like Sonia and Bunny, could only watch and wait for me to give her an opportunity to help.

In the beginning everyone, including myself, expected this phase to pass within a few weeks. Even in my moments of self-condemnation I was sure that whatever evil thing had me in its grip would soon be overcome. The doctor had said that many women go through a difficult period after a hysterectomy. Surely my case was no more stubborn than any other. Time would heal me—time and the Lord.

But as time passed and no improvement occurred, those closest to me began to be worn down by my continuing irritability. I could see the guarded expressions on the faces of my children as they anticipated my next outburst. Even little Greggy was wary of my embrace, so often had he been frightened by my sudden changes of mood. Everyone had clearly had enough of my rotten disposition, but there seemed to be no end in sight.

I think I know when David gave up on me. For more

than a year after my hysterectomy, he tried hard to understand and to tolerate my moods. He demonstrated his caring in many ways—sending flowers for no special reason, calling me every day when he was away, and telling me over and over how much he loved me.

As is frequently the case in a marriage, especially one that has been under prolonged siege like ours, the incident that led to the turning point was a tiny one. It happened one night when David was home and I had gone to bed early to read (mainly to avoid having to talk). That night, playing the role of a loving wife had become too much of an effort. David came looking for me—after praying for me, I'm sure. He had gone to the trouble of making me a cup of tea, something I used to enjoy in the evening before bedtime. He came into the room smiling.

"Here you are, honey," he said, putting the teacup on the bedside stand and seating himself on the edge of the bed beside me.

I didn't even look up from my book as I said flatly, "No thanks, Dave. I don't want any tea."

What I was really saying was, "Please back off, Dave. I'm not in control now. I'm not up to talking and pretending I feel good."

But David heard another message. He heard, "It's no use, Dave. There is absolutely nothing you can do to please me. I am always going to be like this, so stop trying to change me. Go away!"

He left the room without another word, and I heard the cup and saucer clatter against the sink where he dumped them. I cast about in my mind for something to say, some way to apologize. But when the ready tears came welling up, I just turned out the light and had a good cry.

David more or less withdrew from the situation after that. He was polite and kind, but a coolness and distance had entered our relationship. I discovered then just how much my limited adjustment had been dependent upon David's good will and accommodation. When he stopped walking the extra mile for me, I found myself making him the target of my gibes and sniping. I learned that he was most sensitive about being a public figure, and I could easily hurt him by calling him a "big shot" or "Mr. Show Biz." Such thrusts were delivered in a joking manner, but we both knew they were aimed to wound. As my husband packed for a trip across the country, I'd needle him about being such a great blessing to millions while his family sat at home and wondered what he looked like. More and more often, he left tight-lipped and angry. As soon as the door closed, I'd collapse in tears because I had sent him away once more without the support a loving wife could give.

By now it was clear to me that I was a hopeless case. I couldn't stand myself and I was certain that no one else could stand me either. I had managed to estrange my husband and children, and no one—not even God— could break into my emotional prison. I felt that I was losing my sanity. No longer was I the Gwen that David had married, and it crossed my mind more than once that he would be much better off without me. I wondered why he didn't leave me, but David seemed determined to preserve at least the outward appearance of a successful marriage.

David's coolness had persisted for about a month when he invited me to accompany him on one of his trips to California. I should have been pleased, but I was pretty sure that he was just attempting to create the illusion of a couple in harmony. He called it a "second honeymoon," a term that seemed almost laughable to me. Nevertheless, I agreed to go along. If he wanted everyone to think we still had a going marriage, I would somehow summon the energy to make this appearance with him. At least I'd be giving the children and myself a break from having to put up with each other.

Simultaneous Healings

❧

David worked harder than I did to make the flight out to California a pleasant one. He did his best to converse with me about the work that was developing on the West Coast among the hippies, who were then taking over some parts of California. I could feel his growing enthusiasm for this ministry and for his work with the young Jesus people, who were also very visible in those days. Preoccupied with my own misery, however, I made little effort to appear interested or even to comment on what he was telling me. I was well aware of his willingness to throw all his energies into whatever mission the Lord had for him. I just wondered why he couldn't put a similar amount of effort and enthusiasm into our marriage.

The possibility of separation and divorce had entered my mind so often of late that the idea was beginning to look almost attractive to me. If my husband was going to spend the rest of his life taking care of everyone's problems but mine, it seemed that a life apart from him was the only answer for me. With such gloomy thoughts to occupy my time during the flight across the country, I succeeded pretty well in shutting out David and his efforts to make me once again a part of his life and his ministry.

Once we got to the hotel, the tables were turned. David had several phone messages, calls to return, and plans to confirm for the evening. Now I was the one who was being shut out, and I began to seethe silently. I have no idea what finally triggered the argument. I only know that for a few unbelievable minutes David and I were shouting insults at each other, and then suddenly I was all alone. David had stalked out of the room and slammed the door with such finality that I knew he would not be back to take me to the dinner meeting that night.

What will he do to explain my absence to all his friends? I wondered. *Probably tell them I was too tired from the trip. He'll save face somehow and come out of it looking great—the big phony!*

Since there was no one handy to serve as a target for my bitterness, I fumed and plotted the next few hours and finally made the big decision: When I got home to Long Island, I'd begin divorce proceedings. That would show David he couldn't take me for granted! A divorce would serve to tarnish his shining image and show him that Gwen Wilkerson had to be reckoned with. Somehow this decision did not make me feel much better.

David didn't call me or return to the room all afternoon. But about 15 minutes before time for the banquet to begin, there came a soft knock on the hotel door. I opened it, prepared to give David another piece of my mind, and there stood a pleasant-looking gentleman, a total stranger to me. After introducing himself, he told me he had come to escort me to the banquet hall. I could think of no way to decline his offer without being very rude or making a fool of myself. After making a hasty effort to improve my appearance and a mental note to get even with David when the opportunity arose, I left with my escort for an evening I'd not soon forget.

David was to be the keynote speaker at the dinner and after that he was to address a citywide rally at the civic auditorium. When my escort and I arrived at the banquet hall, my husband was already seated at the head table, looking for all the world like a man without a single troubled thought. His apparent lack of concern added fuel to my anger. Nevertheless, I made myself smile sweetly at the people to whom I was being introduced as I was seated at a side table. "He's a big hypocrite, *that's* what he is!" I wanted to tell them all. "He'll get up there and talk about God and everyone will think he's wonderful. No one will know that he doesn't even care about his own wife anymore."

I made it through the dinner by being a good listener. Everyone was glad to tell me what a great man I had married and how happy they were that he was able to speak on the West Coast so often. Biting my tongue to keep from letting them know what was taking place on the *East* Coast while David was away from home, I hoped my silence and my pasted-on smile would lead them to think I shared their sentiments.

Right after the meal was served, David slipped out, as he always did before he was to speak. I knew that he had gone off by himself in order to pray. *He'd better pray,* I thought. *He's going to need a lot of help from God to pull this one off*

Although I didn't note what time David left, I became increasingly aware that he was gone longer than usual. The master of ceremonies was beginning to look a bit uneasy before David finally reappeared to take the podium. *Probably found out that God doesn't listen to a hypocrite,* I speculated, as he began his talk. He appeared to be speaking with no difficulty, however. From time to time, I thought that he was looking at me almost as if in apology.

If he thinks I'm going to forgive and forget how he walked out and left me stranded, he's got another thought coming, I fumed silently. Absorbed in "righteous" indignation and self-pity, I never really heard his message. However, I did hear the enthusiastic applause that followed it, and I even clapped politely myself. When the applause died down, I realized that David had been whisked off to the auditorium where he was to speak again in half an hour. I had hoped to avoid the rally by claiming fatigue, but to do so would have inconvenienced the kind people who were acting as my hosts. I resigned myself to another two hours of exposure to David's public image.

After a short ride, I found myself seated near the front of a large auditorium with perhaps 5000 other people— all of them there to hear a talk on the power and love of God, given by the man I had decided to divorce. Many of the faces around me were young faces—teenagers who were looking for answers to the problems that life poses. They believed that David Wilkerson had some of those answers, and their faces were aglow with expectation and openness. Just looking at them brought me close to tears. How could David introduce *them* to the One who holds the key, when he was unable to find His help for us? Suddenly I was *sure* it had been a mistake for me to come hear him speak tonight, but the program was already beginning and it was too late for me to escape.

What followed remains wonderfully inexplicable. David's talk was aimed at the young people and was a simple message about the love of Jesus. I'd heard him present similar talks before. There was nothing unusual about the words he was saying or about his manner of delivering them. Although I was only half-listening, I watched him with what appeared to be rapt attention. Suddenly I became aware that an aura of light surrounded him. I knew I was seeing a work of the Lord—an anointing of His Holy Spirit on this man whom I was reviling in my thoughts.

How can it be, I wondered, *that the Lord would use him when everything is so wrong in his private life? How can He fill anyone so unworthy with His own precious Spirit?*

Then the Lord Himself gave me the answer to my questions. The glow that surrounded David began to fall also on me and I became aware of the awesome presence of Jesus with me. From head to toe I was immersed in a delicious warmth until all of a sudden I felt completely at one with God.

I knew that a healing was taking place, though I could not guess the profound nature of that healing. I only knew that when I looked back at David he was looking straight at me, and that special spark of recognition was lit between us once again. The Spirit was clearly working on both of us simultaneously. Tears began to find their way down my cheeks and fell unchecked onto my dress, as I began for the first time in many months to praise God for His goodness and mercy.

Moments later, David ended his talk almost abruptly. Forgetting about everyone around me and unmindful of any unseemliness in my behavior, I ran backstage to find my husband. He was running toward the auditorium to look for me, and we met in a crushing embrace. Laughing and crying at the same time, we carried on like a couple of kids in love who hadn't seen each other for months—and really, I guess, we hadn't.

When we finally realized that we were creating a small scene before the startled eyes of the rally team, David took time to say his customary farewells to the appropriate persons. Then, arm in arm and still grinning at each other, we hurried back to our hotel. We could hardly wait to be alone to enjoy our newfound delight in each other. David even took the phone off the hook.

Extending our stay at the hotel for a couple of days, we enjoyed that "second honeymoon" that had eluded us for so long. It was worth waiting for. At first we just rejoiced in the healing of our marriage without trying to analyze what had happened. We knew that Jesus had done for us what we had been unable to do for ourselves—

unlock the door to the love we had for each other, the love which He gave us in the beginning and which had never really died.

By the time we had to return home we had sobered up to the point of being able to talk about our marriage objectively. Both of us recognized that the Lord had given us a new beginning as a gift, but that He expected us now to work *with* Him in order to keep going forward in His way. He made us acutely aware of the many mistakes we had committed in the past year—and indeed in many of the preceding years. We knew that these same mistakes, if left uncorrected or repeated too many times, could unravel our relationship all over again. For the first time *ever,* we began to talk seriously to each other about the responsibility we shared for making our marriage work.

It frightened us both to discover how close each had been to ending our life together.

"When I left the banquet to pray, I was in such a turmoil about our relationship that I decided I'd hop a plane to Mexico and give it all up," David confessed. "I still am amazed that the Lord was able to bring me back."

As I digested this discomfiting bit of news, I told David just how determined I had been to seek a legal separation upon our return to Long Island. "You know, Dave," I mused aloud, "but for the grace of God it could all have ended right here."

"It sure could have," David agreed. "But the same grace that gave us healing is available to help us find the right way in the future. Our suffering during the past year hasn't bccn without purposc. I'm surc thc Lord has a lot to teach us through it. Let's ask Him right now to show us what we can learn from it."

Then and there, we began to pray for God to shed His light on the problems that we shared. The healing begun in Los Angeles was to continue for months. We had a lot of catching up to do.

"I know my illness had a lot to do with our troubles," I told David. "But for the life of me I can't see how we could have avoided it. Wasn't I supposed to have the hysterectomy?" I was truly puzzled, because I felt we had sought the Lord's will in that decision even more carefully than we had before my previous operations. Just why *this* time I lost the battle of recuperation was still a mystery to me.

"I'm not sure we'll ever know just why this surgery was necessary, honey," David replied. "But I'm still sure that we were right to go ahead with it. However, it does seem that we became so accustomed to your being ill that the illness itself became a 'third party' in our marriage. Somewhere along the line I forgot that you were my wife who just happened to be having a series of bad health breaks. I began to think of you as a chronic invalid and I bet you fell into the same trap. As soon as we stopped looking at your illness as a temporary setback and accepted it as a permanent part of our life we allowed it to dictate to our personal relationship. We can't ever let anything—health problems, finances, the children, or my work—take top billing in our marriage again."

I knew David was right. I *had* begun to think of fatigue

and irritability as my masters, something that would always be there determining what I could do and how I would feel. It *was* as though a third party had come between David and me—a nasty, ill-tempered third party, who could ruin everything just by being there.

It was also true that David's work could become another interloper in our marriage if we weren't careful. I had already experienced some jealousy and resentment about that over the years. We would *both* have to work hard to keep the proper balance and priorities in our family life. Still, I knew that David was the Lord's servant. From our first meeting, I had understood that he was called by God for a special purpose. I was sure that the demands of his work would not be a problem for us if I could remember who was the real Head of our family.

Right then I gave David back to God. I realized that in wanting to have first place in his life, I had actually been trying to separate him from his Lord. The result was that I nearly succeeded in separating him from *me*.

We also discussed the decline of my personal devotional life. When I took a hard look at the distance I had allowed to come between me and the Savior who had done so much for me, I was really frightened. I had let the discipline of a lifetime slip away in very short order. David tried to shoulder some of the responsibility for my "backsliding" because he hadn't *insisted* I join him in praying and reading the Word, but I knew that I was responsible for my own actions in this area. It was up to me to keep my priorities straight, and I alone was to blame for allowing that third party of fatigue to dominate my relationship with my Lord as well as with my husband. As David and I asked Jesus to forgive us for not relying more on Him and less on our own resources, I felt with certainty that I would never again cut myself off from His love and strength.

In the months that followed our return home, David and I reserved time at frequent intervals for long talks about every aspect of our lives and marriage. Our talks involved the children, Sondra, my parents, and David's ministry. Every detail of our lives together and apart came under scrutiny as we sought to discover any weak spots in our relationship. Such explorations were hard work and took considerable time, but they were well worth the effort. The Lord showed us what we needed to know and how we could prevent a repetition of the past year's turmoil. At last we were working *together* on our most important investment—our marriage. It was a time of great discovery and growth.

Taking his own advice about not keeping health secrets from each other, David finally shared with me his increasing difficulty with a peptic ulcer—doubtless due in part to the stress he had been under and in part to a tendency inherited from his father. We began to pray with and for each other for physical healing from the One who had already given us such a wonderful spiritual healing.

Our prayers for my physical recovery were soon answered. Gradually the weakness and fatigue left me, and vitality began to return. At the same time, I learned to pace myself better and to accept help graciously from both Sondra and my family. Being all things to all people suddenly seemed less important than taking care of myself so that I could give the best of my resources to whatever opportunities for service the Lord gave me each day.

As we continued to discover new joy in our marriage and our home, David and I were more in love than ever. To be this happy together, this excited about each other after nearly 15 years of marriage, and after coming so close to dissolving that marriage, was truly a miracle. We knew that, no matter where Jesus might lead us in the future, we'd be one in our acceptance of His calling.

This awareness didn't come any too soon, for we were about to find our whole life again undergoing a change of direction. This time God used *David's* health problems to help us discover the new door He was opening to us.

One Step at a Time

As I watched the children cooling off in our small, aboveground swimming pool, I thought more than once of joining them. The hot, sultry day made the idea tempting, but I finally decided it was too much effort to go inside and put on a suit.

The pool had been my suggestion when we returned from California the preceding summer, and David had agreed immediately. Summers were short in Long Island, but those muggy days were gruesome while they lasted. After our own relationship was so beautifully and miraculously restored, David and I both felt a need to give our children more time and attention. The pool was just one of the tangible results.

I had been amazed and delighted to see how quickly all four of the children responded to the change in David and me. Almost immediately after we fell in love again, we noticed a measurable reduction in their anxiety and tension—a reflection, we felt, of their increased sense of family security. Within a few weeks, the petty bickering and vying for attention had almost ceased, and to my lasting gratitude, no one ever reminded me of my past sins of ill-tempered faultfinding. Our total family picture, out of focus for so long, was being beautifully restored by the renewed love between David and me. I praised the Lord daily for this particular miracle of our healing.

Our only remaining problems seemed to be physical ones. David's ulcer still troubled him and I had not yet regained my full strength. I could see steady improvement, however, and I knew that eventually I would be able to take full charge of the household again. In the meantime, how grateful I was that Sondra was still with us!

As if she knew I was thinking about her, Sondra came to join me at the picnic table, bringing a cooling glass of tea in each hand. "If you'd like to take a rest, Mrs. Wilkerson, I'll stay and watch the children," she offered as she sat down in the shade of the umbrella. "Aren't you getting too hot out here?"

I smiled at Sondra as I accepted the tea and declined her offer to relieve me as lifeguard. Once again I wondered what I had ever done to deserve the loyal, efficient help of such a saint. When I thought about the way I had treated her during my illness, I was thoroughly ashamed. Like the children, she had forgiven me and apparently forgotten my spiteful behavior in the past. But I could never forget her patience, kindness, and understanding during that difficult time. It would be impossible for me to repay her. But one thing was certain, she would have a home with us as long as she wanted it, even after I no longer needed her help. She had stood with us during the rough times and she deserved to enjoy this period of smooth sailing with us.

Deciding it was too warm outside even in the shade, Sondra returned to the air-conditioned kitchen to start dinner. I checked to make sure Debbie was keeping a close watch on three-year-old Greggy, and found that Gary had taken over that responsibility while his sisters got out of the pool to sunbathe. *There's another blessing I don't deserve,* I thought, as I watched Gary trying to teach his brother to float. *How many nine-year-old boys would have the patience he has with Greggy?* Gary had always been a cooperative and helpful child and had seldom given me a moment's trouble. Our earlier prediction that he would be the next preacher in the Wilkerson family seemed increasingly accurate. He possessed a deep serenity, based on a relationship with God that was unusual for his age.

"Careful, Gwen," I cautioned myself. "You're beginning to think like a proud mama." Well, I tried not to be *proud* of my children, but I was certainly *thankful* for them. Debbie and Bonnie, both in early adolescence, were growing into lovely young women before my eyes. They still presented quite a contrast to each other, in temperament as well as in looks, but they were good friends and shared a special companionship. They were becoming really helpful to me now and did their best to show me that they no longer needed Sondra's supervision.

Perhaps *they* didn't, but Greggy sure did! Having inherited his daddy's energy and enthusiasm, he was too much for me to keep up with at present. One day, just after I had realized Greggy was missing, Mom called to tell me he was at her house—14 blocks away! He had ridden his tricycle there before I even knew he had left our yard. Without Sondra to help keep an eye on Greggy, it would take all my limited strength just to look after *him*.

David was in Europe again that summer, as his ministry continued to broaden. Much as he dreaded the flight over and back, he had felt a definite calling to respond to an invitation to hold crusades in several major European cities.

The thought of David's travels reawakened my concern about his health. His ulcer was always aggravated by flying, and this year it seemed that he had spent more time in the air than on the ground. Our family physician had warned him that the ulcer could not be treated medically unless he conscientiously tried to avoid stressful situations and got some relief from the pressures of his work. The doctor even suggested that David consider giving up his responsibility of the Teen Challenge Center in Brooklyn. "You'll end up undergoing surgery if you don't ease up!" was his ultimate warning.

I wondered if David had given any thought to this medical advice. He certainly *should* have taken it seriously, since his father's death had been the result of a perforated ulcer. Alarmed at the thought of my husband having a similar condition, I made a mental note to have a long talk with him about his health after he got home in two weeks. We *had* promised to take better care of each other, now that we had found what serious illness can do to a family and to a marriage.

My dad's health was another source of concern to me

now. He had always been vigorous and active. But since he and Mom had moved to Long Island two years ago it seemed to me that he had become increasingly frail and awkward in his movements. Mom worried about him too, but she couldn't get him to a doctor.

We are all a stubborn lot, I concluded. *No wonder the Lord has to deal drastically with us!*

"How soon is dinner, Mom? We're *starved!*" Gary was standing before me dripping as he toweled his hair dry. Beside him, Greggy was wielding his own towel in a laughable imitation of his big brother's actions.

"Ask Sondra," I suggested, giving Greggy a helping hand with his hair drying effort. "Maybe there's time for a light snack first, if you two really think you'll faint from hunger in the next few minutes."

Swim time seemed to be ending now, and with it my reverie. An evidence of my spiritual and emotional healing was the fact that I had come to cherish these relatively quiet times, when I could sort out my feelings and give some thought to past, present, and future developments in the lives of those I loved. Acceptance of my present limitations as down payment on future good health had come when I finally admitted to God that He knew better than I just what was needed for full recovery. My growing vigor was proof of the Great Physician's wisdom.

When David returned from Europe two weeks later, I began to call on Jesus for *more* of His healing power. It took only one look to tell me that my husband was in pain and that the trip had exacted a heavy toll from him.

He was pale and thin and wore a fixed-looking set of creases in his forehead.

He smiled weakly as I greeted him at the door with a welcoming hug and kiss. "Well, Gwen," he quipped, "your white-knuckled flyer is safely home again. Score another victory for modern aviation."

"Cut the funny stuff," I replied. "You look awful, and I'm making an appointment for you to see the doctor. He's going to give you the dickens for not taking his advice to slow down and cut out the long-distance flying."

"I know, honey, I know. But you should have been there to see the way the Spirit is moving overseas. I just *had* to go, you know that!"

"Well—you just *have* to take better care of yourself, or the Lord will be calling home one faithful servant " Praying that my flippant retort wouldn't prove prophetic, I went to the phone to dial our doctor's number. David's appearance had frightened me more than I wanted him to know.

The doctor saw David promptly, examined him thoroughly and, as I had predicted, reprimanded him severely. "I don't suppose it will do any good to tell you this," he sighed as he concluded his examination, "but if you don't stay out of airplanes and delegate some of your responsibilities to other people, this ulcer is going to hemorrhage and maybe perforate and you're going to end up on the operating table."

This was the same warning David had been given on his last checkup, but I could tell that it hit home this time. David began to speculate on the possibility of turning the

Brooklyn Center over to his brother Don and changing our base of operation to the West Coast.

"I can see that my ministry in the future may be centered on those hippies and Jesus people we've been working with in Anaheim," he confided to me. "And then there's another idea that keeps recurring from time to time—a training school for Teen Challenge graduates who want to have a ministry of their own. Maybe the Lord *would* like to remove me from the Brooklyn operation now. This ulcer condition might be reflecting my unwillingness to let go."

We began then to pray seriously for God's guidance concerning our next move. I knew it was hard for David to relinquish the work he had begun in New York, even to someone as close as Don. But soon we agreed that this was indeed what the Spirit was telling him to do. *The Cross and the Switchblade* had witnessed to a far wider audience than it had been expected to reach, and David's flock was no longer just the lost and confused kids in the ghettos of New York. It had become obvious that he could not continue to carry on this wider ministry and still maintain supervision of the Brooklyn Teen Challenge Center.

After coming to this realization, David began laying the groundwork for his eventual withdrawal from the center. It was no easy matter, however, for him to extricate himself from his various commitments in New York. Nearly two years passed before he was finally free of most of his responsibility in Brooklyn.

During this time I watched my father decline in health

until an injury finally brought him medical attention. Once the diagnosis of ALS (amyotrophic lateral sclerosis, often referred to as Lou Gehrig's disease) had been made, it seemed that his downhill course became more rapid. His nursing needs soon grew to be too much for my mother to handle, even with what assistance I could provide. Eventually she and Dad moved back to Forest Hills, where old friends and family members could give her the help she needed.

Before the time came for our move to California, we learned that Sondra would not be going with us. She had become engaged to a fine young man she had met at church. We were her family by then and it was my privilege to help her with preparations for the wedding. After all she had done for me, I was grateful for the opportunity to express some of my appreciation and love for her in this way.

Sondra was married in the summer of 1970, shortly before we sold our house on Long Island. David was eager to get settled into the work that awaited him on the West Coast and he had already found a house for us in Irvine, California. We wanted to make the move by the end of summer so our children could enter their new schools in the fall.

The children weren't altogether thrilled about this move. Debbie would be a senior in high school and she couldn't imagine making friends as nice as the ones she had in Long Island. Even Greggy didn't much like the idea of starting kindergarten without his special pal, Guy. All of the children, however, recognized that David had to go where the Lord was leading him. I talked with them about making it easier for Daddy by demonstrating a willing spirit, and they all responded beautifully.

As for myself, I was not anxious to leave behind the friends we had made over the years in New York. I also felt a growing conviction deep inside me that California was not going to be our permanent home. I said nothing to David about this feeling. California seemed right to him now and I was willing to follow his leading, just as I always had. We could take only one step at a time. But if my hunch was correct, our next step would soon follow this one, and it would be in a new direction.

The Next Step

❧

CHAPTER TWELVE

My hunch did indeed prove to be correct. We lived in Irvine less than a year and during that period I never quite settled in. It wasn't California's fault. We all liked the Southern California climate, our quiet neighborhood surrounded by rolling pastureland, and our contemporary and convenient ranch house with the Spanish-type tile roof. We were comfortable and reasonably happy in our new home, but somehow it didn't have the feeling of permanence about it. I almost felt that I should keep my suitcases packed because I expected David to come home any day and say, "Jesus is calling us somewhere else, honey. It's time to move on."

When I *did* pack my suitcases again, just a few months after our move to Irvine, it was because Jesus had called my father home. I flew back to Pennsylvania for the funeral and remained for a few weeks to help Mom as she adjusted to her loss. When the time came for me to return to California, the pain of parting with Mom was increased by my feelings of guilt. I longed to be living closer to her, so that I could provide her with the comfort and assistance she had so often given me in the past. The best I could do was to make her promise that she would fly out for a *long* visit with us as soon as possible

My state of unrest was aggravated by the fact that David was doing as much flying as ever, in spite of his phobia about it. Travel was absolutely essential to conducting evangelistic rallies and crusades—the type of ministry that was David's special gift. Furthermore, Teen Challenge centers had now sprung up all across the country and even throughout the world. David could not refuse to visit any of them when the support of his presence was needed. His trips back to New York for consultations at the Brooklyn center were made more frequent because the movie version of *The Cross and the Switchblade* was being filmed on the site. To travel across the country by train or bus would be scarcely less arduous, even for David, than the relatively quick trips by air.

Besides, David was trying very hard to spend as much time with his family as possible. Since he could not give up his travels and he *would* not give up his time at home, he seemed finally caught in a dilemma. Unless he could be delivered from his fear of flying, it seemed to me that he would be continually putting his health in jeopardy by subjecting himself over and over again to severe emotional stress. I was sure that the Lord was not through speaking to him about the location of his ministry

When I had a chance to talk with David about my uneasiness, I found that he shared my concern. "You know, Gwen," he confided, "I just don't know *what* the Lord is trying to show me through this phobia. I've asked Him for His healing and hundreds of prayers have been offered for my release from this burden. Often the staff spends an entire flight ministering to me. But my insides always stay tied up in knots until the plane lands. What *does* the Lord want me to do?"

We both knew that God was dealing with us no less in the "bad" experiences of life than in the obvious blessings He sent our way. The Bible tells us that, especially in the promise we so often claimed in Romans 8:28. Our belief that God does indeed bring purpose to the suffering we endure in life had become a deep *personal* conviction after we had been brought, through great tribulation, to a new and wonderful understanding of marriage. So far, however, we had been unable to discover His particular purpose in allowing David's fear of flying and his ulcer symptoms to persist. Obviously, we were not receiving the message He had for us in all of this. Together, we began to pray even more earnestly that the Holy Spirit would open our ears to God's voice. As so often happens, the Lord's answer to our prayers came in a way we wouldn't have chosen.

David had been ministering in Canada and, as usual, had made most of the trip by air. On this particular journey, "the thing which he greatly feared" (to paraphrase poor old Job) seemed perilously close to coming upon him. Bad weather and a rough flight terminated in an emergency landing that was really a close brush with disaster. When David arrived home pale, weak and bent double with pain, his first words were, "Never again! That's *it!* That's the last time I'll ever get into an airplane."

He sounded so positive that I would have believed him if
I hadn't heard him say the same words many times before. This time, however, he emphasized his point by
passing out.

One look at his ashen color sent me flying to the phone
to call an ambulance. At the hospital in nearby Santa Ana,
it was found that the longsuffering ulcer had finally begun to hemorrhage, as our doctor in New York had predicted it would. David had already lost a lot of blood and
the ulcer was still bleeding. Surgery would be necessary
but David was too anemic for an immediate operation.

The next several days were anxious ones. While David
was being prepared for surgery by blood transfusions and
intravenous therapy, the children and I spent much time
in prayer, as did David's staff members and friends. David
and I tried to support each other with words of encouragement and shared prayer, but the circumstances made
it difficult for us to find the peace of God.

The reversal of our previous roles as patient and sym-
pathizing spouse gave both of us new insights. I discovered that I was more frightened for David when his life
and health were threatened than I had been for myself.
David's attitude about the eventual outcome was much
more positive than mine, and he accepted the need for
surgery—but he was *not* a good patient. He was annoyed
with himself for being unable to prevent this interruption
in his work and he could hardly bear the delay necessary
to get him in condition for the operation. The sedatives
he was being given sometimes had the effect of making
him confused, irrational, and even more unreasonable

about his prolonged stay in the hospital. David simply did not have the temperament for being bedridden.

After what seemed endless days of anxiety, the surgery was performed so successfully that it was almost an anticlimax. With the days of waiting and the operation behind him, David was a different person. He told me later that, when he awoke from the anesthetic, the words of I Corinthians 10:13 were running through his mind:

> *There hath no temptation taken you but such as is common to man: but God is faithful, who will not suffer you to be tempted above that ye are able; but will with the temptation also make a way to escape, that ye may be able to bear it.*

David used the days of convalescence for long periods of fellowship with the Lord, thanking God for His faithfulness, conversing with Jesus about His plans for us, and asking the Holy Spirit to show him the "way to escape."

On one of my visits to David soon after the operation, I found him all smiles and eager to talk. Without even waiting for me to sit down, he burst out with, "Gwen, I know where the Lord wants me now! We're moving to Texas, and I will travel from now on by motorbus. What do you think of *that?*"

I thought it was wonderful. It confirmed my own feeling that we weren't through moving, but I couldn't help asking, "Why Texas? What's so special in Texas?"

"It's not what's *in* Texas, honey. It's where Texas is located." He went on to explain to me just how Jesus had revealed His plan to him.

"When I asked the Lord what 'way to escape' from flying He had provided for me, He showed me a motorbus. Then I asked Him how I could avoid spending extra days away from home while traveling that way, and He clearly brought Texas to my mind. If our ministry is located there, I can travel by motorbus to either coast without spending much more time on the road than it now takes to fly across the country. And reaching the central states will be a cinch."

David's excitement and the exertion of trying to share his enthusiasm with me had used up his strength. Lying back on the pillows, he studied my face somewhat anxiously. "What do you think, honey? Are you game for another move?"

I was more than game, I was delighted. When David expressed some concern about his staff's reaction to moving again, I was the one who pointed out that, if Jesus was leading, *He* would take care of that problem. My own insight was that David had heard the Lord correctly.

David was discharged from the hospital within five days after his operation and returned to work two weeks later—much sooner than the doctors recommended. When he told the staff members about his call to Texas, they all agreed to follow where he was being led. Almost immediately, the whole crusade team began to work with David on relocating the ministry to Dallas.

The men went on ahead to find an office, a home for each family, and an appropriate travel vehicle for the crusade team. The ease with which all these details were worked out made us feel more certain than ever that the

Lord was in charge of this relocation of David's ministry.

This time our children were evenly divided, by sex, in their reaction to the move—the boys all for it, the girls much less enthusiastic. Contrary to Debbie's expectations, both she and Bonnie had made many new friends in California and were constantly involved in group activities—swimming, tennis, horseback riding, and you-name-it. Gary, as usual, was ready to go wherever his dad was being led, and Greggy was thrilled to move away from the place where he had had his first encounter with schooling.

Whatever the children's feelings, however, they knew there was no real question about our going where David was called. The Lord's plans might not be *our* plans, but we all knew the importance of following His guidance. Therefore—in varying states of enthusiasm but with unanimous cooperation—the entire Wilkerson family packed up once more to take the next step—from Irvine, California, to Dallas, Texas.

The Promised Land?

CHAPTER THIRTEEN

We moved to Dallas on July 4, 1971—an easy date to
remember. Then followed six years filled with new
friends, delightful surprises, and joyful family milestones.
The move to Texas seemed a rather small act of faith and
obedience when compared to earlier steps we'd taken,
but this time the rewards were prompt and obvious. Not
only did we experience that special peace of the Lord
that comes from following where He leads, we also were
given personal blessings in great abundance. My own cup
was filled to overflowing.

David's work by this time encompassed the entire
globe and reached out to young people of diverse backgrounds with a wide gamut of needs. Because the scope
of his ministry included the hippies, the junkies, and the
goodniks alike, he and his staff prayerfully launched an
entirely new enterprise called World Challenge, Incor-
porated, separate from the Teen Challenge ministry. Immediately the staff grew busier than ever and David's in-
vitations to speak and to hold crusades continued to increase. As the Lord blessed the ministry in many tangible

ways, I was relieved to see David content in his work once again.

With the purchase of the motorbus David had envisioned in his hospital encounter with the Lord, my husband's attitude toward travel underwent a complete change. This vehicle became a comfortable mobile office where he could study, pray, and write. *The Cross and the Switchblade* was followed by *Twelve Angels from Hell, The Little People,* and *Get Your Hands Off My Throat,* and David had many other ideas for books. Travel, which previously had meant time lost in agony and frustration, now offered him long, uninterrupted periods to get these ideas down on paper. And with the stress of flying removed, David became more relaxed, his health improved, and the pain creases soon left his forehead.

The move to Texas also ushered in a new era in our family life. Since David did his best to limit his travel time to ten days per month, he was spending more time at home than he had since our Philipsburg years. The whole family loved it! We were living in another comfortable ranch house in the Dallas suburbs which soon became home base for our four children and all their friends. We enjoyed having the lively confusion of youthful activities around us, and I was thankful to have David's firm hand at the helm during these important years when our three older children were reaching maturity.

Sometimes I found it hard to believe how fast the children were growing up! Bonnie graduated from high school in Dallas, and began to show signs of a talent for writing—especially children's books. Gary had never questioned his calling to the ministry and he was trying to decide which Bible school he should attend following his own high school graduation. Even Greg had come to accept school as one of the hard but essential facts of life and was proving himself a very capable student. It was Debbie, however, who made us most aware of the passage of time. In 1974 she met a handsome young college student named Roger Jonker, and at Christmas they announced their engagement.

As we watched our children managing the transition from childhood to young adulthood without the great upheavals so common to adolescents, our hearts were full of gratitude to God. We had sought His guidance and grace over the years of their growth and He had abundantly provided both. Watching our offspring strike out in new directions with their eyes on Jesus and with faith in His ability to lead them was a blessing unequaled by any other.

The Lord had still more blessings in store for us— although, at first, one of the greatest of these appeared to me to be a tribulation.

Unlike California, Dallas seemed like home to me almost as soon as we unpacked our belongings. Therefore I was not at all interested in moving again. When David first introduced the subject, soon after Debbie's engagement was announced, it was in such an indirect manner that I was caught totally unprepared.

After dinner one evening when the children had scattered in the direction of their own individual interests, David and I were talking about the crusade he'd held the week before. Suddenly he switched to a new topic. "You know, Gwen," he began, "I've always felt drawn to life on a farm or ranch."

So far this was not news. I *did* know of David's love for the wide-open spaces, but country living certainly did not seem to be a serious consideration in view of the kind of work he was engaged in. I made no comment as I waited to see what my husband was leading up to. After a pause he went on.

"Ever since I've been in Dallas, I've had the feeling that a ranch is a possibility for us now—a special kind of ranch." Seeing my jaw drop open, David hastily forestalled the expected protest with, "No, wait, honey. Hear me out."

Realizing that my husband was dead serious, I held my tongue.

David continued, "I've also felt it was time to get on with the dream I've had of starting a school for Teen Challenge graduates where they can be trained for Christian ministry. Then, in the last year or so, the Lord has begun to reveal to me the kinds of things that the near future holds economically and politically. Well—you've read *The Vision*, so you know what I mean."

I nodded. I had read his latest book concerned with the present-day fulfillment of end-time prophecies, but I didn't really see just what it had to do with a ranch.

At last, David got to the point: "I'm beginning to feel a real pressure to consolidate our ministry, to become self-sufficient and free of all debts. I believe the way to do this is to move all of us out to a ranch—the whole World Challenge operation."

I could keep silent no longer. "I take it you've already found the ranch?" My tone reflected the incredulity I felt.

"Well, yes, we have," David acknowledged. "It's located seven miles west of Lindale, about an hour's drive from here. The only hitch is that the man who owns it doesn't want to sell it—yet."

"And didn't you tell him that God wants you to buy it?" I asked, my voice dripping with sarcasm. "*Surely* he knows who David Wilkerson is!"

"Nope, he doesn't—and yes, I *have* told him that I believe the Lord led me there. Now all we have to do is pray and wait."

These last words were spoken with a serene confidence that hardly matched my own frame of mind. Where was Lindale? And who needed a ranch when we were so happy in Dallas? I tried hard to hide my growing dismay, but David knew me too well not to comprehend what my sudden silence meant.

"Just wait until you get a look at it, honey," he offered soothingly. "I know you'll understand what I mean when you see it for yourself."

A few weeks later, when David signed the papers to purchase that 360-acre ranch, both the owner and I were in a state of shock. He still couldn't quite believe he was actually selling his property, and I had not yet comprehended that once again a sign reading "For Sale" had been planted in front of my home.

My first view of Twin Oaks Ranch, just a few days before the sale became final, had done little to reassure me. True, the landscape was picturesque: rolling green hills dotted with ponds and a riot of brightly colored Texas wildflowers. That was *all*, however. The owner was using the property as a catfish farm and lived there in a trailer. Therefore, the land had no buildings or other improvements on it—just a nice view.

Once again, my vision was inadequate. In those raw materials David could see a whole community just waiting to burst forth. As we walked over the acreage, he pointed out where certain buildings would be located.

"There's where we'll put my office, and we're going to make a small pond behind it. The business office will be right next door, and over there we'll have the shipping office and warehouse."

On and on he went, pointing out where the school buildings would be, where some more man-made ponds would be added, and finally the hillside on which our own home would be built, along with smaller homes for our two mothers. Mom was still living in Forest Hills and the only way we could persuade her to move to Texas was by promising that she could have her own quarters, separate from ours. David's mother had been closely involved with his ministry since the New York days, but she too wanted to maintain a life of her own.

As David continued to lay out his plans for the development of the ranch, I began to catch his enthusiasm and his conviction that this was a Spirit-inspired undertaking. By the time we were on the road back to Dallas, I was as excited about our future home as he was.

After the purchase of the ranch, events moved so rapidly that it was a long time before I had a chance to ponder how I felt about anything. Our house in Dallas sold much more quickly than we had anticipated. Since our home at Twin Oaks was at that time merely a blueprint, I found myself supervising the move from a comfortable, seven-room house to a 58-foot trailer on the ranch property. Most of our household goods had to go into storage—and I soon discovered that the items most in demand by our family were those I had consigned to the warehouse.

Soon after we moved into the trailer, Debbie and Roger were married in Dallas. Their wedding took place on our twenty-third wedding anniversary—June 14, 1975. Debbie and I had great fun planning that lovely event, and the shared shopping expeditions and trips back and forth between the ranch and Dallas served to draw us even closer in those final weeks before my firstborn child became a bride. Debbie's big day was perhaps a bit more elaborate than my own wedding had been, but it was no less meaningful. And David and I made certain this time that there would be no scarcity of photographs to record the happy occasion.

Before I had time to feel the letdown that normally follows a wedding in the family, I was up to my ears in blueprints, room designs, and samples of carpeting and drapery materials. David himself had planned the decor of our home while I was busy with wedding preparations, but he asked me to collaborate with the wife of our ranch manager in decorating the dormitories, classrooms, and guest quarters for the school. When these tasks were completed, there were flower gardens to be planted around our home and throughout the ranch. It was a busy time for me but I thrived on it!

Within an unbelievably short period, the ranch blossomed forth with the ponds and buildings David had described to me on my first visit, and Twin Oaks became a bustling, thriving enterprise of many facets. In June of 1976 the first students arrived to enroll in the Twin Oaks Leadership Academy. That same summer, Debbie and her newly graduated husband joined us at the ranch where Roger had accepted a position on the school staff. Our first grandchild, Brent Dean Jonker, was born on October 30, 1976. My delight in having this newest family member within spoiling distance was greater than my shock at suddenly finding myself married to a grandfather.

I don't suppose any period of my life has been as enjoyable as this wonderful six-year interlude after our move to Texas. Gone were the days of feeling "out of it" or "on the shelf." I was now able to share in my husband's work without sacrificing a bit of my important role as mother and homemaker. The Lord even allowed me to fulfill, on a small scale, my adolescent dream of becoming a beautician. For years I had been giving haircuts to David and the children, and now I was able to be of some service to the students in the school by giving free haircuts in the ranch barbershop.

As in those earlier years in Philipsburg, I was ready to remain right where I was for the rest of my life. It was tempting to think that I had been led by God into my own little promised land. Life certainly seemed full of milk and honey, and I was growing rather used to having it that way.

Just as I was on the brink of taking it all for granted, the Lord intervened again and made it clear that some more refining, some rougher polishing, would be necessary to prepare me for His kingdom. The "promised land" turned out to have its share of deep valleys too.

Why Me, Lord?

CHAPTER FOURTEEN

The steaming shower felt so comforting on that chilly January morning that I lingered under the warm spray for a few extra minutes. The Christmas holidays had left me a little tired, but my weariness was far outweighed by a deep feeling of gratitude for the many blessings our family had enjoyed together during that holy season. The thought of our grandson and the joy that a sweet new baby brings to Christmas brought a smile to my lips and a prayer of thanksgiving to my heart.

Just then my soapy fingers encountered an unfamiliar hardness in the midst of otherwise pliable flesh. My smile faded and my forehead creased with concern as I tried to rediscover the tiny nodule that had just aroused my body's alarm system. There it was again—a definite lump, no bigger than my fingertip, just under the skin of my left breast. In its firmness it resembled the breastbone adjacent to it.

Since it wasn't painful to the touch, I was tempted to ignore it. "Probably not worth the worry," I told myself. But I probed and manipulated the offending nodule a bit longer.

Ever since my cancer surgery 13 years earlier, I'd been careful to examine myself regularly for any unfamiliar lumps anywhere on my body. By now such explorations were a well-established practice performed almost unconsciously. So much time had passed since that first operation that I no longer worried about the possibility of a recurrence. Still, I knew that a woman should be careful. Recent surgery for breast cancer in the wives of the president and vice-president of our country had focused national attention on the importance of self-examination. The mere thought of that disease made me feel sick.

"Oh, come on, Gwen!" I reprimanded myself sharply as I turned off the shower and stepped into the folds of a fluffy towel to dry. "You know you've never felt better in your life. So you're a little tired from all the holiday festivities. Who *isn't?* You don't feel the same fatigue and weakness you experienced when you had cancer."

Catching a glimpse of my reflection in the steamed-up mirror, I had to admit that the face staring back at me certainly looked healthy. *I have been feeling great,* I reminded myself, cheered by the thought that even simple colds had been infrequent in recent years. My health had never been better.

I looked down at my body, flushed a rosy color from the hot shower. Grinning, I said aloud, "The old girl really doesn't look bad for 45." I finally concluded that such a little bump was nothing to worry about. Nevertheless, as I finished drying off and started to dress, I made a mental note that I must keep the promise David extracted from me 13 years ago by telling him about it without delay.

Just as I knew he would, my husband became instantly alarmed when I told him that same evening of my discovery. His concern took the form of a barrage of questions: When had I first noticed it? How big was it? Did it hurt? Why hadn't I told him?

When he finally gave me the opportunity to answer, I pointed out that I *was* telling him at the first opportunity and that I felt it was innocuous.

"Well, maybe it *isn't* anything important," he replied in a calmer tone, "but I'll feel better when Dr. Rice says so. Make arrangements to see him tomorrow. Promise?"

"Sure," I agreed readily. Dr. Jack Rice, the ranch physician, was a close friend as well as our family doctor. It would be much easier to ask his advice about this little problem than to consult a total stranger.

To my relief, Dr. Rice agreed that the lump didn't appear to be anything more serious than a small cyst. "It will probably dissolve spontaneously and disappear within a few weeks, Gwen," he said by way of reassurance. "However, you must promise me you'll watch it closely for any change or any growth. Can't be too careful with breast cysts, you know."

At bedtime that night, David and I prayed together for a prompt disappearance of the annoying nodule and from then on I tried hard to pretend it wasn't there.

When January came to an end, the lump was still present. It hadn't gotten much bigger but I couldn't kid myself that it was shrinking. Dr. Rice felt that a consultation was in order and arranged for me to be seen by a gynecologist in Dallas.

This doctor all but stood me on my head to examine me. When he was done probing and prodding me from every conceivable angle, he recommended a biopsy removal of the nodule so that the cells could be studied under a microscope. "I think you ought to have it done immediately, Mrs. Wilkerson," he urged. "You won't have real peace of mind until you know without doubt that the lump is benign."

I wasn't so sure. That tiny cyst didn't scare me nearly so much as the thought of another surgical procedure. A lot of years had passed since my last operation but time had not changed my feelings about hospitals and surgery.

I held out for almost a week before David and Dr. Rice convinced me that this was merely a minor bit of diagnostic work that would be worth the discomfort for the reassurance it would provide. "Well, OK," I said at last. "But I'm not going to have it done before Tuesday. I sure don't want to miss the Valentine banquet Monday night." The students at the school had planned this event themselves as a love gift for the staff. February 5 promised to be a gala evening, and I was determined to be there for it.

That party proved to be the best possible antidote for the anxiety that was beginning to build up inside me. Among a batch of hilarious skits that were part of the entertainment was one that purported to show how David and I *really* act at home. That bit of nonsense gave me the merry heart that "doeth good like a medicine," and the spirit of fellowship and love that pervaded the whole affair set me free from morbid fears. As I tumbled into bed late that night, I had scarcely a thought for the next day. "Wasn't that *fun?*" I asked David as he turned out the light. "What a great bunch of kids!"

The next morning, after casually telling our family that we were going to Dallas for the day, David and I drove off for my appointment with Dr. James Chisom, the surgeon recommended to us. Only Dr. Rice and Barbara Mackery, David's personal secretary and my good friend, were aware of the nature of our mission. It seemed unwise to worry our family and friends unnecessarily. By the end of the day our fears would be laid to rest. This was a small personal matter, to be dealt with privately.

Dr. Chisom was a calm professional who gained my confidence immediately. He agreed that the lump looked innocent enough, but he also agreed that it should be removed and identified. "It appears to be very superficial, Mrs. Wilkerson," he assured me. "We can excise it right here in the office under local anesthesia and have the lab look it over. The whole matter can be resolved in a few minutes."

Since that was the purpose of this visit, I submitted docilely to being sedated, draped, scrubbed, and anesthetized with a shot of Novocain into the area from which the lump was to be removed. Now that the moment had come, I was calm and confident. David was waiting just one room away, keeping a prayer vigil, and I knew that Barbara and Dr. Rice were also in prayer. Why had I put off this simple procedure so long? It was much better to face the problem head-on and deal with it. I would trust the Lord with the results.

I knew that all was not going well when Dr. Chisom took so long to free the tiny piece of tissue. "It's not quite so superficial as it seemed," was his matter-of-fact explanation. As the five- to ten-minute procedure he had promised was prolonged for half an hour, my anxiety increased with each passing minute.

I later learned that David too became concerned and, on the spur of the moment, called Dr. Rice to join us. His explanation was that he felt I might be relieved to see our medical friend after it was all over, but the truth was that David himself really needed Dr. Rice's reassuring presence.

At last the surgery was completed. The nurse chatted amiably with me as she placed a small bandage over the stitches. "There now, that wasn't so bad, was it?" she asked with a smile. Relief began to replace my earlier fears.

In less than 15 minutes Dr. Chisom entered the back door of his office with the pathologist's report. One look at his stricken face told the story. I hardly even heard his words, "I'm terribly, terribly sorry, Mrs. Wilkerson, but it *is* malignant."

I wish I could say that I reacted with calm acceptance, but I didn't. My whole being rejected with horror the idea of another cancer, and I cried out, "Oh no, not again! Why *me*, Lord?" Then I began sobbing uncontrollably.

Immediately David was through the door and by my side. His arms encircled me tightly as we wept together.

After all those years of good health, another cancer to battle! For the moment, we just couldn't accept the fact that it was happening to me again.

From the depths of my despair I heard David's voice, ragged with emotion, praying aloud. As he continued to hold me before the Lord, my sobbing slowly died away and I began to feel the Spirit moving in my shattered life. Very quietly, very gently, the pieces were being picked up and put back together.

By the time I had completed dressing I was dry-eyed and calm, even though my mind had not stopped turning over the ugly facts. There would be more surgery—disfiguring and devastating in its implications—and I would have another uphill fight to recover health and stamina. Furthermore, Dr. Chisom could give me no guarantee that surgery would be adequate to stop the disease that threatened me. It was entirely possible that nothing could be done at this point to spare my life.

Even as these thoughts came to me, however, a sense of peace and assurance was taking root in my spirit. "Lo, I am with you *alway*," my Lord had said, and throughout my life I had found Him to be faithful to that promise. "Jesus is Lord," the Spirit was reminding me, "and He can be trusted."

All around me plans were being made quickly, almost frantically. I heard my distraught husband arrange for a private room so that he could spend the night on a sofa by my side. And I listened carefully as the doctor explained that a mastectomy would be scheduled for the next day. But none of this had much of an impact on me. My calm acceptance finally got to David and he blurted, "I don't know how you can take this all so well. Here I am, going to pieces, and you sit there as though nothing is happening."

"I can't believe it myself, Dave," I answered him quietly. "But somehow the Lord has given me a sense of peace about what is to come. I know it won't be easy, but He's going to see me through it."

My surgery was scheduled for Wednesday at 11 o'clock. That seemed an awfully long time to wait when David and I awoke in my hospital room on Wednesday morning. By an unspoken agreement, we didn't discuss the details of the surgery that Dr. Chisom had carefully explained to us the day before. The morning was unusually bright and beautiful for February—the kind of day for optimism and cheerful thoughts—and we began it with prayer and praise. Holding hands, we asked the Lord's blessing on the surgery and praised Him for His hand upon my life. Then I asked David to read to me from the Word.

Turning at once to Psalm 118, he began, *"O give thanks unto the Lord; for he is good..."* Words of comfort and of life filled my thoughts as he read on: *"I called upon the Lord in distress: the Lord answered me, and set me in a large place. The Lord is on my side; I will not fear: what can man do unto me?...I shall not die, but live, and declare the works of the Lord."* The concluding verses of this psalm—*"Thou art my God, and I will praise thee: thou art my God, I will exalt thee. O give thanks unto the Lord; for he is good: for his mercy endureth for ever"*—did more to ease my mind than the preoperative sedation that followed. After that we waited together in silence. Words were no longer necessary.

As the effects of the anesthetic slowly ebbed away, I became increasingly aware of a searing pain in my chest and a relentless throbbing in my left arm. It was impossible to ignore the obvious assault that had taken place on my body. I felt a sudden shudder of revulsion as I recalled that I was now something less than a whole woman. The argument that only a piece of flesh had been removed did not really comfort me. I was grateful for the life-sparing skill of the surgeon, but I shrank from the disfigurement that was the inevitable result of his work. "Why me, Lord Jesus?" I asked again, as I shut my eyes tight to stop the tears. "Why *me?*"

In His Strength

I must have been daydreaming as I cleared up the remains of breakfast, for I didn't realize that David was out of bed until I felt his hands slide around my waist and heard his low "wolf whistle" in my ear. "Hello there," he said softly as he nuzzled the back of my neck. "And just what is a beautiful woman like you doing in my kitchen?"

"Idiot! You startled me!" I protested, laughing as I turned to give him a peck on the cheek. "How late did you stay up?"

"Oh, it must have been 1:30 or 2 o'clock. I got into writing up the newsletter and just couldn't quit till it was done." David's night-owl habits were now so well established that everyone in the family took it for granted he would turn in hours after the rest of us. Part of this time alone he always spent with the Lord, but he also managed to get a great deal of work accomplished after midnight. Instead of arguing with him about the crazy hours he kept, I simply allowed him to sleep as late as he could on the mornings he was at home.

"I like that color on you," he said approvingly as I fried his egg the way he liked it. I was still getting the old "once over" as I slid into the chair beside him to keep him company while he ate. "How come you keep getting better looking every day?" he asked between mouthfuls. "Don't you know that a gal who's been through what you have isn't supposed to look that good in slacks and a sweater?"

"And don't *you* know that a preacher who's been married to the same woman for 25 years isn't supposed to come on so strong and seductive at this hour of the day?" I retorted.

At that we both laughed out loud and then just sat and grinned at each other.

Oh, Lord Jesus, I asked silently, *how did you manage to put my life back together so well in just six short months?* Here I was bantering with David in our old lighthearted fashion, knowing that my husband found me attractive and desirable in spite of the mutilating surgery I'd been through.

As if he had been reading my thoughts, David suddenly took my hand and said, "We've come a long way, baby. Who'd have believed it possible back there in February?"

The recovery phase after the mastectomy *had* been rugged. In spite of the excellent attention provided by David, the hospital staff, and devoted family members and friends, the Lord and I fought an uphill battle against pain, weakness, and a sense of hopelessness that threatened to unravel me completely.

One of the Lord's allies in this battle was a wonderful

woman from Reach to Recovery, a group formed to help rehabilitate mastectomy patients. Composed of women who had been through the ordeal themselves, this national organization has a realistic, no-nonsense approach without being unsympathetic or harsh. Mrs. Ott called forth my fighting spirit as she explained how hard it would be to do the necessary exercises at first and how long total recovery would take.

"Well, we'll just see about *that,*" I told myself as I set out to master seemingly impossible maneuvers with my left arm, and to learn all I needed to know about those absurd-looking prostheses that would help restore my figure to normal under my clothes. Because my operation had been a "simple mastectomy," which left muscles of the chest and arm relatively undisturbed, my physical rehabilitation was rapid. Scarcely three weeks after the surgery I had regained the full range of motion in my left arm, and the swelling and discomfort had almost disappeared.

Emotional recovery, however, lagged far behind the physical. At first it seemed impossible that I could ever adjust to the loss of a part of my anatomy so bound up in my thinking with femininity and sexuality. On the second postoperative day, Dr. Chisom arrived at my bedside and announced that he was going to remove the drain,

"What drain?" I asked in surprise. I had no idea what lay under the mountain of white gauze that covered the operative site.

"The one we have hidden under here," he answered as he began to peel away layer after layer of bandage.

Removal of the last few layers and of the tiny rubber drain just about killed me, but I forgot the pain when I got my first glimpse of the incision.

"Oh, dear Lord!" I cried. It was even worse than my worst imaginings. Not only was the familiar mound of flesh gone, but in its place was an actual concavity with a bright red, swollen incision running across it. It was the ugliest thing I had ever seen.

I shut my eyes quickly and turned my head as Dr. Chisom ever so gently redressed the area. Praying hard for control, I managed to hold back the tears until I was alone again. When David returned to the room, however, I was sobbing like a child, and I couldn't even tell him why.

Oh, Jesus! I cried inwardly. *I'm so ugly now. How will David ever stand to look at me again—let alone hold me or caress me? I'd rather be dead than to be undesirable to him. How can I bear it?*

I was convinced at that moment that any physical intimacy with David after my recovery would be out of the question. I knew my husband and what pleased him. *He'll be completely turned off,* I concluded, *and I don't blame him.*

What I failed to consider was the Lord's compassion and His understanding of *all* the details of married life. He had instituted this union of man and woman, and He had gone to great lengths in the past to ensure that our particular union would last. Still I did not dare to hope for the beautiful miracle He was already beginning to work in my husband.

Five days after the operation, I returned to the ranch and to a tumultuous welcome staged by the entire staff and student body. Signs with greetings and Scripture verses were fastened to the trees along the road to our house, and my friends lined up along the way to wave, whistle, shout, and blow horns. At the house a luncheon awaited me and my family, and a beautiful new chaise lounge was there for my comfort—a "welcome home" gift from David. A queen at her coronation never felt more feted or loved.

It *was* good to be home. I had missed my children, my mother and, of course, my grandson. Being with them again buoyed my spirits, and I felt a rush of gratitude to the Lord for the wonderful people He had placed in my life. Thanks to their thoughtfulness, I never lacked for attention at any time during my convalescence.

I was still uneasy about my future relationship with David, however. He had canceled out on one crusade while I was hospitalized—the first time he had *ever* sent the team out alone to hold meetings at which he was scheduled to appear, but shortly after my return home he had to leave for another crusade. I really didn't mind his going. I still needed a great deal of rest, and twice a day in those early days of convalescence, fluid had to be aspirated from the incision. It was only right that he should get on with his work and leave me to recover at the pace nature decreed. Still, I was too insecure to be totally comfortable with the idea of his being away from home. I began to wonder if he had guilt feelings about leaving and about the secret relief he must have felt at getting away from the deformed parody of a wife I had become.

While David was away, I slipped into deep depression. Only the persistent prayer and ministry of my dear friend Barbara kept me close to the Lord during that bleak period of time. Finally I was able to seek His face on my own behalf. "Oh, Lord Jesus," I prayed then, "if David feels guilty *now,* how will he feel when the bandages come off? He hasn't even seen me yet. Please give me the strength I need to face him." I did a lot of praying while David was gone, and Jesus did a lot of comforting.

A few weeks later, the last of the tape and gauze was dispensed with and I could dress normally with the help of those clever prostheses. David was at home again, as eager as ever to wait on me and pamper me. But we had not yet had our "moment of truth."

That came when David walked in on me one evening as I was undressing for bed. There was an awkward silence as we both realized we were facing a test. Mustering all the courage I possessed, I turned slowly toward him and anxiously searched his face for the slightest hint of rejection.

I didn't find what I was looking for. Instead, sheer love and admiration were etched into every line of his expression. As he took me in his arms he said softly, "You are a beautiful woman, honey," and I knew immediately that this was no pretense, no act put on to spare my feelings. The Lord had actually given David new eyes with which to see me. To him I was as much a woman as ever. Our relationship, even the physical, has only improved since that moment.

"Wake up, Gwen," David said, touching my arm to bring my wandering thoughts back to the breakfast table. "You need to decide if you're going with us to Colorado next week. Are you feeling up to it?"

"Oh, sure," I replied with confidence. I'd already made a couple of trips with him in the last few months and felt stronger each time. "My energy level seems back to normal now," I assured him.

"That means you need only *one* nap a day instead of two or three," he teased. Then his expression turned serious and he looked anxiously into my eyes as he asked, "You're sure you're feeling OK? No problems you haven't told me about? I can't help wondering what you might be keeping bottled up inside you."

I knew what was really bothering him—the fact that I had refused cobalt treatments and chemotherapy in spite of Dr. Chisom's recommendation that these be given as a precaution. My surgeon had been quite frank with me after the operation. "So far as we can tell, the surgery was a success," he explained. "We excised all the diseased tissue we could see. However, there is always the possibility that cells we could not see might have invaded surrounding tissue—even under the breastbone. Because of that possibility, I'd advise radiation and anticancer drugs. That way we can be more sure of success." He told David the same thing.

The problem for me was that no one could say positively that additional treatment was necessary, or that it would be effective if it *was* needed. The one thing they could tell me for certain was that such therapy would produce unpleasant side effects.

Ultimately the decision was mine, but David and I discussed it thoroughly and prayed for guidance from the Lord before I said no. "I don't want to lose you now," was David's way of saying, *"Do* it!"

"I'm not afraid of dying, Dave," was my response. "The thought of going to be with the Lord is a lot more appealing than the idea of prolonging my illness by treatments that might be either unnecessary or ineffective."

" Are you *sure* you're making the right decision?" David persisted.

"Of course not, honey," I answered. "I'm not *sure* of anything when it comes to my health. I'm not sure why all this happened to me in the first place. And I certainly am not sure about what tomorrow might bring. I can only live one day at a time. *Today* I don't feel that cobalt treatments or drugs are what the Lord has in mind for me. Perhaps He'll give me different guidance in the future. We'll see."

And there the matter rested. Now David in his mind was questioning this decision again as he asked me if I really felt as well as I seemed to.

"Yes, Dave, I feel fine," I assured him. "I promise I won't keep you in the dark if there is any change at all. We've learned our lesson on that score, haven't we?"

"We *should* have," Dave replied, rising as he spoke. "Gotta run now, Gwen. I should have been at the office by nine. Please take it easy on the housework. I want you to go with me to Colorado."

With that and another kiss, he was off and running. From the window I watched the clouds of dust chase his car down the road to his office. With another surge of gratitude, I thought, *What a lucky woman I am to have David as my husband!* Then I began to thank the Lord for that blessing and for others that crowded into my thoughts faster than I could name them: good, caring parents to begin with; healthy, attractive children; friends like Sonia, Bunny, Sondra, and Barbara who had enriched my life and helped me over the rough places; and now this lovely home, a fine son-in-law, and an adorable grandson. *And just maybe the child that Debbie is carrying now will be a little girl for us to cherish,* I mused.

Even as I enumerated these many tangible blessings, however, I was aware that they have merely been the frosting on the cake. The best part, that which has given meaning to the rest, is the presence of the living Christ in all of my experiences. Without Him none of the other blessings would have been possible. Unless my mother had introduced me to Christ early in my life, I would never have found David so irresistible. Without the healing touch of the Lord, my marriage as well as my emotional stability most certainly would have failed. And who can say what effect *that* would have had on the children?

"Thank you, Jesus, for being my anchor," I said aloud. "If you hadn't sustained me through all the sickness and long battles to recover, I wouldn't even be here today to tell my story."

As I pondered anew the Lord's love and His grace, I

was forced to conclude that I have learned only one "secret" along life's pathway—just one simple "answer" to the question of how to live successfully in this world. That secret is to live every moment of every day *in HIS strength*.

~ PART TWO ~

The Story Continues

CHAPTER SIXTEEN

My book entitled *In His Strength* included events in my life up to and including most of 1977. I had told my story as honestly as I knew how, even rewriting the ending when my breast cancer was discovered. Twenty-four years have passed, and in June of 2002 David and I will celebrate 50 years of marriage and ministry together! Our marriage is crowned with the comfortableness and contentment enjoyed by those in seasoned relationships who have weathered the vicissitudes of life together. We constantly rejoice in the goodness and blessings of the Lord toward our entire family.

As I ponder all that has happened in the past two decades, I can see how God developed my ministry and character in *seasons*. When our children were at home, I was totally committed to my calling as a wife and mother. Once the children left home, however, God surprised me when He called David to start a church in New York City. Once again I was a pastor's wife, a role I thrive on because it allows me to minister to people on a very personal level. I realized that God's timing is so unquestionably perfect. He has filled our lives with joy, while at the same time we have gone through fiery trials that have purified us and deepened our bond with Him and with each other.

Let's pick up the story toward the end of 1977...

— 🌸 —

After my surgery for cancer, David and Dr. Rice persuaded me to submit to a short course of radiation in spite of my personal desire to forego further treatment. They correctly reasoned that it couldn't hurt me and it *might help.* "Do it for your family, Gwen, if not for yourself." The four treatments were over before I knew it and the holidays were upon us.

The Christmas season is always a happy time for us and that year was especially joyous. The whole family— four generations strong, including David's mother and mine, our five children (counting our son-in-law, Roger), and our 14-month-old grandson, Brent—gathered at our home at Twin Oaks Ranch to celebrate the birth of our Lord Jesus. I remember it as being one of the best family gatherings ever!

Three days later, Debbie had her second son, Matthew Landon, and now we had *two* grandbabies to love! The year 1977 was ending in much better fashion than it had begun. Cancer and disfigurement were all but forgotten, and the new year dawned full of promise and hope.

Our lives were filled with blessings and a sense of well-being the next few years as we continued to enjoy good health and growth unmarred by trauma. The children matured and made defining changes in their lives, marrying spouses who shared their godly values. Nothing gladdens the hearts of Christian parents more than seeing their offspring establishing homes where Jesus Christ is honored. Only Greg, who was 16, still lived at home. I was surrounded by love and was feeling healthier than I had in years. I actually began to relax and believe that life would be easier and less hectic now that the children were growing up and our nest was emptying—but I was wrong!

— 🌸 —

"Mom, can you come right over?" I could hear the distress in Debbie's voice when she called me that cold morning in late March of 1981. "I've got this awful pain in my side. I can't even stand up and I'm afraid to lift Matthew."

As I hurried the short distance to her house, I assured myself that my daughter was just experiencing muscle spasms, but when I saw the tears streaming down her face, I knew she was in trouble. I immediately called David at his office because I was more alarmed than I wanted Debbie to know. My heart was filled with fear at what her pain might mean.

"I'm sending Roger right home," David responded without hesitation. "Debbie needs to get to a doctor and he'll want to take her." Roger held a demanding and responsible job at Twin Oaks Academy, but David was his boss. Roger was home in a matter of minutes.

We were hopeful that Dr. Rice's examination would discover something superficial but his findings heightened our concerns. He ordered some tests for Debbie, and then advised her to see a surgeon right away. As Roger repeated the doctor's urgent opinion that Debbie should not delay getting the tests done, echoes of my medical history began replaying in my mind. Two days after Debbie's initial examination, she was in a hospital in Tyler, Texas, being prepped for surgery.

After finding someone reliable to take care of Debbie's children, David and I kept vigil with Roger in the surgical waiting room. We were hoping and praying for good news, but my heart was gripped with fear. *"Lord, please! Let this be a false alarm. Let them find something totally harmless in there."*

Sadly, this was not to be. The surgeon appeared exhausted and defeated when he came looking for us after nearly four hours of surgery.

"I'm so sorry," he said, shaking his head. "We had to take quite a bit of her colon out, but I believe we got it all. It's hard to understand a cancer like that in someone so young."

I felt myself go cold all over. *Cancer—colon cancer.* The same diagnosis I had been given after my first surgery. *"Why is this happening all over again, God? Is this my fault? Did I pass this disease on to my daughter? Oh, God, help me to trust You. Give us all strength. Teach us faith, patience and endurance. Help us not to waver, Lord."*

We were all in a state of near-shock. David whispered encouraging words about God's goodness and His power to heal, but I could see tears in his eyes. Roger looked like someone had kicked him in the stomach. And me? Well, I broke into tears and cried openly, unable to contain my gricf and fcar. I was so frightened for my daughter and her two young sons. She was only 27! How could this be happening to her?

Within a week of the surgery, as my beautiful firstborn child lay in her hospital bed, heavily sedated for pain and desperately fearful of her chances for recovery, the doctors brought more bad news. She would need powerful chemotherapy to give her the best chance possible to fully conquer this disease. The medical team recommended M. D. Anderson Cancer Center in Houston as a good facility for administering the combination of drugs she would require for her chemotherapy.

We all gathered for prayer and agreed that we felt Debbie should go for the chemo. After all, she was very young—and her family needed her. Who *wouldn't* grasp at any help God provided, even if it came in the form of powerful chemicals? There was too much at stake to leave any stone unturned in her treatment. As soon as Debbie was strong enough to travel, Roger drove her to Houston and checked her into the hospital where the *real* ordeal began.

— ❋ —

"Are we going to lose her, Lord?" I stared in horror at the skeletal body curled in a fetal position on the hospital bed and silently screamed at God, "That can't be my Debbie lying there. What have they done to my little girl?"

The drugs that were being pumped into Debbie's bloodstream to fight the cancer cells appeared to be killing off the rest of her body, as well. She seemed to shrink right before our eyes in a matter of days.

David and I had arrived in Houston the day after Debbie had been admitted to M. D. Anderson. We were there to love our daughter and her husband and to offer prayer support and encouragement. We also needed to assure ourselves that she was in good hands. We could feel the prayer support of family and friends and were so thankful for it. David cancelled one crusade to be at the hospital with us, but eventually he had to leave to take part in other meetings. I remained in Houston, staying at a nearby hotel, and Roger was constantly at Debbie's bedside.

I tried so hard to remain positive in the midst of a desperate situation, but it was not easy. To tell the truth, I was pretty angry with God. It was one thing for me to go through cancer surgery myself, but watching my daughter suffer was much worse for me. I would have given anything to trade places with her. All I could do was hold her hand, stroke her dry, feverish brow, whisper words of love and encouragement, *and pray.* Half the time I couldn't even tell if she heard me, but I knew God was listening.

Roger was always near and remained surprisingly strong for a young man facing the possibility of losing his wife. The prospect of bringing up two little boys without their mother to nurture and care for them must have been daunting, but he showed no fear or anger. All I saw was his unwavering strength, and faith in the mercy and healing power of Jesus Christ. When he spoke at all of the future, it was only in terms of "when she is well again." His serenity and confidence comforted me and I tried hard to believe with him that Debbie would be healed. She just *had* to get well!

The anticancer poisons being given to Debbie were gradually tapered off and signs of life returned to her ravaged body. She was terribly thin, but she had survived the treatments! After a month of hospitalization, she was released to return to her home at Twin Oaks. There was a great celebration and many prayers of thanksgiving at the ranch when Roger carried his very frail wife into their home.

In spite of round-the-clock nursing care and the prayers of Christians worldwide, Debbie did not recuperate well. She remained pale and complained of constant stomach pain the first few days she was home. When she began to vomit blood, Roger once again rushed her to the hospital in Tyler. There they found the source of her hemorrhaging—a perforation in her stomach wall. The toxic drugs used in her chemotherapy had literally eaten a hole in her stomach. In a little over three months, Debbie had undergone two extensive surgical procedures and two courses of debilitating chemotherapy—and she was sicker than ever!

I was in prayer one morning when I received a worrisome call from Roger. "Mom, can you come to the hospital *now?*" he asked in a voice that was uncharacteristically guarded. When I assured him I could, he added quietly, "She's not responding to treatment, Mom. I think you should come as soon as possible."

Now I *was* alarmed! It was not like Roger to sound so troubled and disheartened. I was afraid of what I would find when I got to Debbie's hospital room.

After hanging up the phone, I sat alone in the house—David was traveling in crusades. First I wept with a sense of weakness, remembering Roger's voice, "...come to the hospital *now.*" I already had my Bible open to the Psalms and as I leafed through the Word, I asked the Lord for encouragement and hope.

My eyes fell to my open Bible and the words of Psalm 100 leapt off the pages at me. How many times I had read that particular portion of Scripture, but that morning in my kitchen, it stopped me cold. My eyes filled with tears of gratitude as I read of His faithfulness.

Make a joyful noise unto the Lord, all ye lands. Serve the Lord with gladness: come before his presence with singing.

In spite of my anxiety, His directive to "shout joyfully" seemed strangely appropriate. As I pondered the first verse, I quietly asked the Lord, "You want me to be *glad,* don't You, Father?"

Know ye that the Lord he is God: it is he that hath made us, and not we ourselves; we are his people, and the sheep of his pasture.

He reminded me that He had made us and we didn't have anything to do with it. He is worthy of all praise—at all times, whether we know what He's doing or not.

"Lord," I prayed, "You formed Debbie and made her perfect, so I praise and thank You, Lord. Help my unbelief."

Enter into his gates with thanksgiving, and into his courts with praise; be thankful unto him, and bless his name.

"Lord, I will enter into Your gates with thanksgiving and praise. I bless Your name, Lord; You have been so good to us," I whispered.

Before I knew it, I was giving praise to my Lord. I felt His presence empower me and I jumped into the car and rushed toward the hospital. Tears flowed down my cheeks but I hummed as I drove, *"Great is Thy faithfulness...morning by morning new mercies I see!"*

Over and over I repeated the words of Jesus, "Fear not—I am with you! Fear not—I am with you!" God came into that car and flooded my soul with His presence, bringing peace and assurance. All my fear disappeared and I knew that He was working endurance, steadfastness and patience in me, according to James 1:3. My spirit resounded with the truth, *"God is in control!"* and I knew that no matter how many miles separated me from Debbie, He was ministering healing to her.

The sight that greeted me when I rounded the corner to Debbie's room took my breath away. My precious daughter was sitting up in bed sipping broth that the nurse was offering her, and her cheeks were beginning to show the first hint of color. She greeted me with a big smile and stated the obvious, "I'm feeling much better, Mom!"

Recognizing that I was witnessing *another* of God's miracles, I exclaimed out loud, "Thank You, thank You, Jesus! You never fail!" What joy and gratitude filled my heart.

That was the turning point in Debbie's recovery. In talking with her later, we realized that she had begun to rally while I was praying back at the ranch, and she steadily improved. Within a few days she came home to stay— weak, and still in need of nursing care, but definitely on her way to complete health. Our praise and thanksgiving to the God Who heals continues to this day—every day!

A Leap of Faith

All too quickly, it seemed, David and I found our "nest" totally empty. We were blessed to have Debbie and Roger and their boys, as well as our two mothers, living close to us, but after all those years of bringing up children, we missed the activity and youthful vitality in our home. I soon realized that God was allowing us this new freedom in order that we could more easily follow His direction in our lives, no matter where He led us.

David had held rallies in New York City *every* summer since first going there in 1958. Even after we moved away in 1970, he returned year after year with the crusade team to conduct evangelistic services for the people of this great metropolitan area. Living on the ranch had taken David out of New York City, but it had *not* taken his love for the city's people out of *him*. I was with him in New York for one of these summer rallies when God did a marvelous work in his heart.

"What's the matter, Dave?" I mumbled sleepily as I heard my husband roll out of bed and start to move around the hotel room. "You haven't been to sleep, have you?"

I already knew the answer. He'd been tossing and turning ever since we'd gone to bed and now he was up, fumbling around in the dark, opening and closing drawers.

"I can't sleep, honey," he responded from the shadows. "I'm going to get dressed and go out for a walk. Sorry I woke you." Within minutes I heard the door open and close as he slipped quietly out of the room.

I knew David was agonizing over the tremendous increase in the severity of the problems he was seeing on the streets this year. Homelessness, which in the past had been a problem for only the most desperately oppressed in the city, had suddenly become an overwhelming problem. It was no longer merely the alcoholics and drug addicts who were unable to provide housing for their families. Many of the formerly "working poor" had lost their jobs and were also seeking shelter wherever they could find it. The number of beggars and panhandlers in Times Square was astonishing.

A new plague called crack cocaine had appeared on the drug scene. It was ravaging lives in ways that made the heroin problem of previous decades pale by comparison. The gang-mentality that David had encountered among the city's youth when he first began Teen Challenge thirty years earlier was gone. In its place was an attitude of "everyone for himself" that produced a vicious disregard for anything or *anybody* that stood between an addict and his drugs.

I recognized the restlessness growing in David and I knew it was because the hopelessness of the people was eating away at him. Depravity was all around us and I sensed that his heart was breaking. This was not the first night he had been sleepless, nor was it the first time he had taken a late-night walk to pray and seek the Lord's will on how to reach the lost souls all round us. I tried not to worry about him out on the dirty, crime-infested streets, but I usually spent the rest of the night praying for his safety until I heard him come back into the room. This night was no different.

The clock read after 4 o'clock when David returned. It was still dark outside, but morning was coming fast. I was exhausted from lack of sleep, but he looked energized.

David glanced at me to see if I was awake, which I was. "Gwen, honey," he began, "I've just had an incredible talk with the Lord, and I have something very important I need to tell you." *Right at that moment I knew!* I think I had seen it coming for quite some time, but at that moment the full picture zoomed into clear focus in my mind.

"We're moving back to New York, aren't we, Dave?" I asked quietly, before he could go any further. "The Lord wants you back here to minister again, doesn't He?"

David's face registered surprise—then relief. "Yes, we're coming back to the city. I've been praying so long that the Lord would raise up someone with a strong word for these people, someone who will build His church here in the midst of all this sin and decay. The more I've prayed, the more convinced I've become that He seems to think *I* am the one to do it. I *have* to say 'yes' to Him."

Even through my fatigue I put forth my best effort to respond with enthusiasm, "Of *course* you do, Dave." As the words left my mouth, the peace of God entered my heart and my questions and fears disappeared. I knew that I was in perfect harmony with my husband's decision and his leap of faith for New York City. I even began to feel stirrings of excitement and anticipation deep within me. Moving back to New York was *not* what I had ever imagined we would be doing when our children were grown, but somehow it just seemed *right*. That is one beautiful thing I have learned about our loving heavenly Father: When you yield your will to Him, He surrounds you with His perfect peace. As in the past, the Lord arranged it so that His call to David was met by a quiet assurance in my own spirit. We were a team—and we were in this together!

—— 🌸 ——

David and I returned to Texas with our minds filled with hopes and plans for following the call of God to New York City. I reflected on my *first* move to New York many years ago, remembering how terrified I had been. I was no longer that naïve young mother, but I knew I still needed His strength and guidance as much as before.

Family and friends reacted to news of the move with enthusiasm, and some of his staff—like his personal secretary, Barbara Mackery, and her husband, Jimmie—were ready to get packed and moved right from the start. World Challenge headquarters would remain in Texas and Roger, our son-in-law, would stay behind with his family and continue serving as business manager of the work.

David and I, along with Barbara and Jimmie, went to

New York City in early 1987 to search for suitable housing for our two families. We needed a sizable facility to rent for worship and David wanted to be as close to Times Square as possible. We were able to reserve a couple of condominiums in a building under construction, and David selected Town Hall Theater at 43rd Street and Broadway as the place where "Times Square Church" would hold its services.

David always intended to launch this church by calling *new* converts to Jesus, but when the first services were held in October of 1987, the congregation was comprised of a cross-section of the city's population. Many were already committed Christians who had been praying for years for a church of this type in midtown Manhattan.

On the second night, two to three hundred people had to be turned away. We had run newspaper ads prior to our inaugural services, but it was the word-of-mouth news that David Wilkerson was back ministering in New York that seemed to generate an incredible response. From the very beginning, spiritually hungry people streamed into Times Square Church to hear God's Word proclaimed.

Within three months it was evident that a larger auditorium was needed, so we moved to the Nederlander Theater at 41st Street and Broadway. But even with a seating capacity much greater than that of Town Hall, this auditorium was also packed from the beginning. The Lord continued to bless Times Square Church with increase. That's when David and his World Challenge board decided that the ministry should have a *permanent* home.

In March, 1989, David and his board purchased the Mark Hellinger Theater at 51st Street and Broadway—the theater where "Jesus Christ Superstar" premiered and had a long run. Thousands of people from the heart of New York City and beyond came to worship. Eventually three services were held each Sunday, plus three midweek services, so that nearly 7,000 persons could take part each week.

Our ministry certainly grew far beyond anything I had envisioned as God used Times Square Church to reach out to hurting people. At one point, He led us to open "Sarah House," a ministry where women with drug or alcohol addictions, abusive partners, unplanned pregnancies, and children needing support can be housed and cared for as they recover and become self-supporting. The Lord also led us to minister to men with life-controlling problems. And through the grace of God and His wonderful provision, we have been enabled to serve meals to the hungry—as many as 150,000 meals a year.

We were truly humbled to see how God utilized our smallest efforts, producing a great harvest of fruit from the tiniest seeds of faith and trust. I thought we were taking a great step of faith in returning to the city, but we were really only taking baby steps of obedience. The *real* force and power came from above and we were about to go through an ordeal that would prove His power once again.

The Best of Times —
The Worst of Times

God was multiplying His blessings in and through Times Square Church and His hand was on our family in a wonderful way. We were being blessed with more grandchildren and our cup was *running over!*

There was only one little cloud on the horizon during that time and it hovered over Bonnie. She and her husband, Roger Hayslip, had moved to El Paso, Texas, to work with the homeless and her health had deteriorated to the point that her doctor recommended a total hysterectomy. Bonnie desperately wanted another child and this news was a real blow.

Finally, in 1991, Bonnie relented and a date was set for her surgery. I made plans to go to El Paso to be with her and her family and even stay with her after she returned home. But this was not to be. A very short time before her scheduled operation, I discovered a lump in my breast. For fourteen years I faithfully and carefully paid attention to my health. *Fourteen years!* And now I discovered something that was not right. I knew I shouldn't ignore it, so at the most inopportune of times I made an appointment with my doctor.

The doctor tried to placate me when I told him I wanted a biopsy. "I'm certain it's just fibrous tissue, Mrs. Wilkerson," but I wasn't at all reassured. He finally said, "Well, a biopsy is certainly easy enough to arrange and you'll be relieved to know that you don't have to worry about it anymore."

But I *did* have to be concerned about it, because the biopsy—just like the first one fourteen years earlier—revealed malignant cells. So instead of flying to Texas to be with Bonnie, I checked into Cornell Medical Hospital in New York City to have my remaining breast removed. More than being frightened, I was angry and disgusted. This was my fourth bout with cancer and I wondered when the battle with this wretched disease would be over.

Even with my husband's heavy schedule, he was always with me when I needed him. His support was so vital! When a man finds out his wife has breast cancer, his reaction is a major factor, an inestimable tool to give her courage. Many men just can't handle it and I can only imagine the added anguish a woman goes through when that happens. How thankful I am for David and his unconditional love. He was rock solid in his belief that God would see me through once again, as He had in the past. The morning of surgery, he prayed for me but we also prayed for Bonnie, who was to be admitted to a hospital in Texas the following day.

The surgeon appeared in my room and asked, "Are you ready?" I nodded 'yes' and he responded, "Well, let's *go*, then!"

It took me an instant to realize that he expected me

to *walk* into the operating room and climb up onto the table. I was stunned by his "request" but I complied without comment. I felt like I was on automatic pilot by this time; what was the point of questioning anything? Anyway, I was concerned about my daughter, and as my anesthesia was taking effect, my last thought was of her. *I wonder how Bonnie's holding up. I sure wish I could be with her.*

The day of my surgery was pretty much a blur, but Bonnie was on my heart. The next day I asked about her and David told me her surgery had gone well—and then he quickly changed the subject. "Just relax and take care of *Gwen,*" he answered. "You need time to mend now."

For the first couple of post-surgery days, I struggled with the discomfort of my incision. I took painkillers and slept as much as I could, but I was fighting back a feeling of uneasiness about Bonnie. I wanted to believe David's reassurances, but I was afraid there was something he wasn't telling me. I perceived just the slightest hint of evasiveness in his answers.

By the third day I *had* to know the full story. "Tell me what's happening with Bonnie," I demanded of David when he came in to visit. "*Is she okay?* I've been so worried about her."

David's eyes were bright with tears as he struggled to respond calmly. "They found cancer in her uterus, Gwen. She's really sick and very scared. They're planning to start her on radiation as soon as she is strong enough, then chemotherapy and cobalt treatments."

I felt like screaming, "God, no! Not Bonnie, too! This

is more than I can bear." Instead, I maintained my composure and said as calmly and resolutely as I possibly could, "Then I am getting out of this hospital and going to her. She is not going to be without our help at a time like this!" Nothing the doctors or my family said could dissuade me from leaving the hospital and catching the first available flight to El Paso. When David saw that arguing with me was useless, we headed to the airport together.

I have asked Bonnie to share her testimony in the next chapter.

Bonnie's Story —
In Her Own Words

CHAPTER NINETEEN

On a hot, sunny April day in El Paso, I was alone at home taking care of the usual household duties. My husband, Roger, was at work and our sons were in school. I had undergone a rather routine medical procedure a week before and had not yet received the report of the findings. I expected to get the customary postcard in the mail advising me that everything was normal. Instead, the telephone rang and the voice at the other end of the line delivered the most devastating news I could have imagined hearing. "Bonnie, your test results just came back and I want you to see an oncologist immediately. *You are full of cancer.* The biopsy shows endometrial cancer with possible spreading to the cervix." I had never dreamed I would hear such bad news *over the telephone* and I was rocked to the core of my being. All I heard was *"You're dying of cancer."*

I walked around the room in a daze, hardly believing what I had just heard. *What should I do? Whom should I call?* "Oh, God, help me!" Not five minutes after the phone call, I heard the welcome, familiar voice of my husband, who was home from work early, "Where are you, Babe? I'm home!" I fell into his arms and I could tell he was startled by my appearance. "Bonnie! What's wrong? What's happened? Is it one of the boys?" Roger, always the strong rock of our home, held me tightly as he tried to get an answer out of me. "I have cancer! I have cancer!" I repeated it over and over, dozens of times, and each time I said it I became more frightened. Even though Roger held me close and wouldn't let me go, I sensed that this was the first time that even he couldn't help or comfort me. I was facing this battle on my own and I knew it.

April 28, 1991, was a very long day, indeed. After Brandon and David got home from school, I wouldn't let them or Roger out of my sight. My thoughts the rest of that day were only questions: *Am I going to die? I'm only 36 years old. Will I be around to mother my children? Can the boys handle this bad news?* I dropped into a deep hole that felt like the valley of the shadow of death, and each day I lost ground.

I had served the Lord all my life, but now I was trembling, facing a trial for the strong in heart. I wanted a playground but here I faced the front lines of harsh reality, a battle for the mature. I knew only the great in faith win this type of war and I felt neither mature *nor* strong in faith. I even talked to God about it: "Please, dear God, not this road, *please.* There's a road over there I know I could handle much better. I thought You said You would only give me what I can handle. Lord, I'm looking at my feet and I *know* I cannot walk this road. *And I will not walk it!"* Imagine saying 'no' to God!

After dealing with my initial fears and letting some of the truth slowly sink in, I knew that the only thing that could really comfort me that night, besides the Lord, was the voice of my mother. But at that very moment, she was lying in a hospital bed in New York City awaiting surgery for breast cancer. I didn't want her upset before her surgery, because she had enough to deal with, but I knew I had to tell Dad somehow. My heart was heavy for him because he had had to deal with cancer so many times before. First my mom, and then my sister, and now his other daughter. I felt I didn't have the strength to tell him on the phone, because I knew if I heard his voice, I would lose control. I didn't know what to do, so I did nothing that night.

My brother-in-law, Roger Jonker, now worked in the New York office, so the following day I called and shared the news with him. Roger immediately told Dad, who was in his office, that he needed to meet with him privately. When he told Dad that I had cancer, his response was, "Cancer! Not again. Not my other daughter, too. Not now." My dad agreed that it would be best to withhold the news from Mom until after her operation. Dad knew it would be very difficult to keep anything from Mom—it would be like telling General Patton that no war was going on. I've always thought of Mom as a spiritual General Patton when it comes to suffering. She doesn't crumple in the face of adversity—she fights it! And that's why I had to have her. I needed her near me with her strong spirit to tell me, "Sweetheart, we will get through this. Hold tight—and TRUST THE LORD."

Mom is tough and it's hard to fool her. After her surgery, while she was still recovering, her inner radar went off and she asked Dad, "What's wrong with my Bonnie? Something's wrong with my Bonnie. I just know it. Tell me, Dave, right now!"

Dad couldn't evade Mom's persistent questions any longer, so he folded her in his arms and told her, "Gwen, Bonnie has cancer. Her tests came back and it doesn't look good. She has uterine cancer and they think there's a chance it may have spread to her lymph nodes!"

Mom insisted on calling me right away and what a relief it was for me to hear the voice I had been longing to hear, finally! I cried and cried as she talked to me, and I was cradled in a calm assurance that God would be with me—every minute of my ordeal. After I hung up the phone, my shoulders straightened up and I was ready to fight. General Patton had imparted to me her fierce resolve to fight to the end and she had included instructions on how to win the battle—through our faith and trust in Jesus.

Mom went into action right there in her hospital room. Regardless of her bandages and IV lines, she was determined that she was going to get to El Paso and she was planning her trip. She knew God would give her strength to get to me and she put actions with her faith. That is what has always amazed me about my mom—her faith in God is always rising to the occasion. God seems to have complete trust in her to be able to handle all she has been given, and in turn, she has complete trust in her God to see her through. God also knew His little Gwen would be the key to my surviving the fear of cancer.

My operation was on May 7, 1991, and one look at my husband's face after surgery told me everything. He looked horrible, but he stroked my hair and told me how much he loved me. Some of our closest friends were in the room and they all looked terribly sad. Roger told me, "Your mom and dad are flying down from New York," and I immediately knew that my cancer must have spread. This was something I didn't want to hear but something I would hear for months to come.

My dad had sent me two dozen yellow roses to remind me how much I was loved. I found out later that Mom had a hard time during the flight down. Dad told me she cried quite a bit, but she never lost her confidence in what she knew God would do for her daughter.

I had a highly skilled, experienced doctor with a terrible bedside manner. After he operated on me, he told my husband, "She's full of cancer and she's never going to make it. It's all through her body—she's dying." The doctor spat out these words with all the matter-of-factness of a robot. No wonder Roger's face looked so drained. Mom would end up being sorely tested by this clumsy, seemingly unfeeling doctor.

I will never forget the moment Mom and Dad walked into the room. Finally I had just what the doctor ordered: the comfort of my husband *and* my parents. Immediately after Mom fussed over me and held me, she took over the hospital room. I laughed as I watched her fix my bed and make sure the nurse was doing her job. (Our whole family thinks she would have made the best nurse in the world.) She also became my bouncer. When I was too tired to visit and the room became too loud and busy, she "lovingly escorted" people out.

When Mom heard how the doctor had so callously told Roger the news of my condition, she was horrified. Believe me, she was anxious to set this man straight. "How dare he tell my daughter there is no hope?" *(General Patton again.)*

Whenever Mom needed rest, Dad would convince her to go to my home and take a break. I observed Dad through my pain medication and naps and I saw the pain on his face. How many times had he seen this picture—looking over at a loved one lying on a hospital bed facing the same battle? I'm sure if he weren't a praying man, Dad would have felt helpless. Even with his faith, it was still hard. People don't realize the heartache unless they have been there.

My doctor learned very quickly that his bedside manner would have to improve around my mother. She is no fool and she is very straightforward—no mincing of words with her! My radiologist, Dr. Anarupta Gupta, was a different story, however. Mom was very pleased when she walked into the room.

Dr. Gupta, a lady from India, was very intelligent and matter-of-fact, but she was also nice and congenial. I liked her immediately and thanked God for her under my breath. She would end up being a very stable force throughout my ordeal. She sat down with Roger, me, Mom and Dad and explained my cancer and my treatment. Things were mostly a blur for me, but I distinctly heard, "If Bonnie doesn't have treatment, she will not live." Those words hit hard! The treatment consisted of six months of radiation, six months of chemotherapy, and three days in the hospital for cobalt treatment. This last treatment would be in total isolation. I saw tears in Mom's eyes. Dad held Mom, Roger held me, and God held us all! Nonetheless, it was a very difficult moment.

Mom and Dad had to return to New York after their short stay. They had both been so good to us and we hated to see them leave, but they needed to get back. They agreed with Roger that I would need help in the house, and we thought of a dear, tenderhearted woman named Ann who had helped Mom at one time. When I called her, Ann said she would pray about it and let me know immediately. When she called back and said she could come out and help us, we were all thrilled and relieved.

After my parents returned to New York and the day before I left for M. D. Anderson in Houston for a second opinion about my treatment, I fell into a very dark pit. Actually, I gave in to fear and gave up my fight, surrendering to defeat. I couldn't eat, my shoulders rounded into a slouch, and complete despair overtook me. That night Mom called and when she recognized my state of mind, she really gave me a good talking-to. Mom is a very down-to-earth lady and even though she is tender and gentle in spirit, she can be very strong and forthright.

"Now, Bonnie, you have to get your fight back. You have to trust God through this! He is with you every step. Remember His promises! You have a wonderful husband

and two beautiful boys who love you and need you. Now you straighten up and get yourself something to eat!" *Yes, General Patton!* I obeyed my mother and made it through the night—then I thanked God for such a strong mother who knew how to pray.

The doctors at M. D. Anderson Cancer Center agreed with the other doctors' diagnosis, prognosis, and recommended course of treatment. My radiation would be administered in El Paso and was scheduled for June. Mom flew back down for much of the time and my wonderful sister-in-law, Teresa, and her baby daughter, Alyssa, also came to be with me. It helped so much to be surrounded by a loving family. Mom, as usual, kept everything moving smoothly at home. She cooked and cleaned, cared for Brandon and David, and drove me to and from the cancer center, making sure I was as comfortable as possible. And remember, she was still recovering from her own surgery!

The radiation treatments made me very weak, and I could eat only certain foods. Mom made delicious mashed potatoes almost every night—and my house was never cleaner!

Dad encouraged me when he called by telling me that everyone at Times Square Church was praying diligently for me. My dad really "stood in the gap" for me with his many prayers. I received hundreds of cards and letters from all over the world because of his mailing list, and these got me through many tough days.

After I finished radiation treatments, Dr. Gupta scheduled me for the cobalt implant. I had no idea what this was, but I just wanted to get through it. Mom never left my side. She had been there for my radiation and she would be there for my cobalt implant. Dr. Gupta told me that I would be flat on my back for three days after the cobalt was surgically implanted in my uterus. I wanted to be prepared so I packed some of my dad's teaching tapes, some music tapes, my big, black Bible, and some stationery. I was planning to have a wonderful time being brave before the Lord. I was going to show God, my family, and the nurses just how strong I really was. After all, I was my mother's daughter! How desperately mistaken I was—I had absolutely no idea what was to come!

When I opened my eyes after my operation, I saw that my legs had been elevated and I was unable to move my body. Because of the way I was tilted, I would not be able to sit up at all—and I was to lie in that position for three full days. To make things worse, the nurses could come in for only five minutes at a time because of the high level of radiation in me. They told me even Roger and Mom could visit me only ten to fifteen minutes each day—and they were taking a chance.

Mom had a lot to handle when she got to the hospital that day to visit me. My door had radiation warning signs all over it and her heart dropped when she saw me lying on my back filled with dangerous radiation. I could never hide anything from Mom and she knew right away that I wasn't doing well. I hadn't touched the tapes and stationery, of course, and there was no inspiring music playing in the room. Mom knew I was frightened and in pain, and I knew that all my hopes of being a valiant patient were crushed. The reality of the situation hit us both very hard that day.

When Mom saw my intense fear and realized that I had given up, she began to pray. She couldn't even hold my hand because she wasn't allowed to touch me. They allowed her to stay with me for ten minutes, but it felt like ten seconds. She knew that her walk out the door would be terrible for me, but I cannot imagine how devastating it was for her. She wasn't able to be my caregiver and act as my nurse this time. She had to walk away and leave me in the hands of the Lord. Only later did I find out how truly traumatic it was for Mom, because she was strong for me and never showed her fear and grief.

By the third night I felt like I was losing it. I felt every arrow the devil shot at me and I couldn't even say the word "Jesus." I was truly in the valley of the shadow of death, thinking God had left me alone. I hadn't slept the previous two nights and I wasn't allowed to take any medication that would help me sleep. I looked over at my little mountain of tapes, my Bible, and other things I had brought. I had thought I would be able to minister to myself and to the nurses who flew in five minutes at a time. I just rolled my eyes and thought what a dumb idea that had been.

I was able to turn on the TV, but when I did all I saw were programs with normal people who didn't have cancer. This was the longest night of my life. I could not sense the presence and comfort of Jesus at all. I told myself, "He doesn't care about me." My doubt had to hurt the heart of my Lord.

By 3 o'clock in the morning, I wasn't getting better, I was getting worse. I begged the nurse for a sleeping pill. "Please! I haven't slept in three days. Help me, please!" As soon as the nurse left, the telephone rang and it was Kelly and Gary, who always gave me encouraging words of comfort. "Bonnie, God woke us up to call you and tell you that He loves you. If you can't talk to Him, just say His name. He understands. Let Him love you."

It was so good to hear from Gary and his wife, Kelly, and when I hung up the phone, I did what they said. "Jesus," I said faintly. Nothing more than that—just "Jesus." Well, He wasn't gone after all. He was with me and I could feel Him holding me. All of a sudden, I felt like a queen and for the first time throughout this whole ordeal, Jesus was my everything! He was my nursemaid and my caregiver. He suddenly showed me a side of Him I had never seen before. He orchestrated a miracle for me right then and there. He carried me that night in His arms and I slept like a baby. From that night until this very day, my eyes have been open to the shepherd heart of God. God stood with me in the fire of my soul that night.

Chemotherapy was next for me—six months of it— and once again Mom would fly in and out to be by my side. We talked a lot in our time together and discussed how God works in the lives of different people, especially women. I have read many biographies of women missionaries, strong women of God who have made a difference in many lives, who are looked upon as godly heroes of the faith. Many women have spoken of their sacrifices overseas and included stories of jungle living and starving people. These saints of God deserve our admiration and respect, but I notice that we rarely praise and admire those who have suffered in body. Many people don't realize that the calling to a life of physical suffering is just as fruitful as those who are called to Africa and beyond. Instead, they are told that there is sin in their lives or they lack faith. After walking the road of physical affliction and experiencing His powerful, healing touch, God showed me something that I had never realized before. Multitudes of lives have been touched for His kingdom because of my suffering, as well as the suffering of my mom and my sister, Debbie. While it is not a road I would have chosen, He chose it for me. And through our pain, we have tapped into the world God travels most—the road of suffering.

After I was through with my treatments, Mom and I had quite a few good laughs as we read some of the advice we received from so-called well-wishers. Mom has a great sense of humor which I'm thankful I inherited.

"Mom, listen to this one. This person says I should try a coffee enema. I don't think so! I'm already hooked on Dr Pepper."

"Mom, did you hear this one? You're sick because you have sin in your life." How was that supposed to encourage or comfort me?

One day a "well-wisher" called me and said ever so politely, "Don't worry, Bonnie. When you die, God will send a good wife for your husband and a good mother for your boys." I called Mom in New York because this time I wasn't laughing! "Mom, can you believe what that person said?" Mom, being the practical realist that she is, said softly, "Honey, just ignore it!" That's all I needed to hear and I never thought about it again.

It has been ten years since I was diagnosed with deadly cancer and God has completely healed me. I can honestly say that I am richer for the trial. Little did I know that the valley of the shadow of death had treasures in it for me—treasures of learning more of God's caring, nursing character, and in the midst of it all having a treasure with me—MY MOM!

Abiding In His Strength

❀

When David and I arrived in El Paso, we went straight to the hospital. Roger and some of their close friends were there. We had asked Roger to have the doctor wait until we arrived to give Bonnie her final diagnosis, but the doctor had already been in.

"Daddy, I'm going to die, aren't I?" Bonnie had always been a "daddy's girl" and as soon as he walked into the room, she cried out to him.

"There's no reason to think that, honey, because God is in control. That's just Satan trying to tell you there's no hope, but there's hope in Jesus. You're not going to die; God won't allow it."

We understand that sometimes God does allow people to die, but at this time David had strong faith that it wasn't Bonnie's time. I had stood back while she talked to her dad, but then she saw me.

"Mother!" I went over and hugged her. "You're going to be fine, sweetheart," I assured her. "God is with you." Then we cried together. It's amazing how God sent His strength to all of us at that time.

Bonnie's husband, Roger, is a remarkably strong man and he stayed very close to her. He was always tender toward her and became a rock she could lean on. Her boys were her lifeline during her entire ordeal. "I can't leave my boys. I can't leave my boys," she said over and over.

Bonnie has already mentioned the horror of her cobalt implant, but I'll add my reactions. I was totally unfamiliar with cobalt treatment; in fact, I had never heard of it. I was out in the hall when I saw a huge machine coming toward me and my heart immediately went out to the person who was going to have to be treated with that monstrous piece of equipment. I started praying for the patient herself, and for her parents. I have so much compassion for the mothers and fathers who watch and wait for their sick children to get better. As I silently prayed, I saw the "monster" being wheeled into Bonnie's room and that was it! I started pounding on the wall, almost wailing, "Jesus! Jesus! Help us, Lord. *She can't go through that*. Please, Lord." I was so mad at God right then—but I still cried out to Him.

It's important for me to convey to you, the reader, that we all have human reactions to human conditions. I strongly identify with parents who see their children go through deep trials. But as soon as we cry out to God, *He assures us of His presence and strength*. When I cried out to God in that hospital hall, He held me up and kept me going.

During Bonnie's cobalt ordeal, Roger and I always had to be in white, sterile gowns whenever we went into her room. After she completed her treatment, Dr. Gupta said to me, "Your daughter is so different." I guess a lot of women lie there screaming and carrying on. Even though Bonnie wanted the cobalt block out more than anything in the world, her behavior during an excruciatingly difficult time made a great impression on those around her. She was a witness without even realizing it.

After those last horrible three days, Bonnie came home and did well. For ten years she has had routine check-ups with no recurrence of cancer. She is perfectly healthy and her bubbly, joyful personality still radiates to those around her.

That year also brought a sad loss for our family. When David and I moved to New York, my mother and David's mother had remained in Texas, but we saw them as often as we could. Occasionally when I was with my mom I would ask her if she was in pain and she would answer, "Yes, my back hurts." We thought it was arthritis and for several years that's how we handled it. She loved being independent and making cookies and Italian delicacies for her grandchildren and friends, and she stayed active.

At a family event, it was evident that she was suffering more than a backache. I called Dr. Rice right away and he had her admitted to a hospital in Mesquite, Texas. Tests and x-rays revealed a very serious problem—colon cancer! Dr. Rice and two other doctors gave us the news, and then asked, "Should we operate?" Mom was 95 years old and my initial response was "No."

Mom had always dearly loved David and he was there at her bedside. "Mom, you don't want to go through this surgery, do you?"

"No, David, I don't. Whatever you think—whatever God tells you," she answered. So that settled it.

I had to fight feelings of guilt for not getting my mother diagnosed sooner. I felt so bad, but I just had to leave it with the Lord. Mom knew how much I loved her—I had always been her little girl and we shared a precious, special bond. With David by my side, I felt more confident in making decisions concerning her care and addressing the doctors. We decided to take her directly from the hospital to our place up north. At that time we had the big coach bus, so we bundled her up, got pain medication for her, and made her as comfortable as we could on the couch in the bus. We drove straight through and got her all set up with a hospital bed and round-the-clock nursing care. About six weeks later, her family was sitting around her bed singing Christian choruses, just watching and waiting. We knew her time to go was near. She tried to open her eyes, but then she just slipped away…to glory!

Times Square Church continued to grow and thrive spiritually as the uncompromising Word of God was taught to the congregation. Outreaches to the homeless and hungry, to single mothers and their children, and to widows and addicts were established. God sent us good, committed workers to implement the different facets of these outreaches. We were winning battles on Satan's territory and we faced many obstacles, which we overcame in the name of Jesus and by the power of the Holy Spirit.

As is true in any endeavor undertaken for the Kingdom of God, Satan tries to stir up trouble. The Bible warns that our enemy comes to kill, steal, and destroy. This happens on the mission field, in the local church, and in para-church ministries—and Times Square Church was no exception. When one particularly painful episode occurred, David was devastated. As he poured out his sorrow to his Father and sought Him for guidance, I felt for the first time in our marriage that I could be a comfort to him. He had been a wonderful husband and it was finally my time to really support and encourage him. I am so thankful that by the time this happened, the Lord had done so much in me that I was able to really stand strong as we faced this situation together. Again, God was our unchanging anchor and brought us through in great victory.

— 🌸 —

Today David preaches in front of thousands and writes all the newsletters for the ministry; he also provides leadership for Times Square Church and World Challenge. I fulfill a silent, behind-the-scenes role and that is the way I prefer it. I love reading the thousands of letters that come into the office. I don't read them out of curiosity but because I feel the spirit of the writer. The Lord speaks to my heart and I often weep as I pray for the precious people who take time to write. I send as many personal notes as I can and sometimes I make phone calls and pray with people personally.

My heart is especially touched by letters from the elderly. Many of them are lonely, but most of them are sad, holding on to God for their children and grandchildren. They are so faithful to pray for their families and I rejoice that I can pray with them. I love it when they write back to tell me, "It is so good to know that you are praying with me. Thank you!" Even though David and I are no longer the young people we were when we first came to New York City, many of the elderly seem to think of us as their children.

Many people live in fear of cancer and think they can't handle it, but I can testify that God is present every step of the way. I am aware that some of His precious children do not survive cancer, but I am able to share from firsthand experience that God brings many through to glorious, perfect health—for His glory! Satan is a liar and he tries to defeat us before we have even begun to fight.

One question that occasionally jars me when I read it is, "Is the Wilkerson family cursed? Why do you think your family has gone through so much sickness?" Until I see it in print, I never even think of such a thing. Far from being cursed, our family is blessed beyond measure. The peace of God always comes to us by His grace, no matter what we are going through as we daily abide in Him. I have found that His peace is not something that comes from the mind to soothe the spirit, but from the Spirit to soothe the mind. The words of Andraé Crouch's song, "The Blood Has Never Lost its Power," says, *"...it reaches to the highest mountain and it flows to the lowest valley."* We have found that to be so true, so let me say it again, "We are blessed!"

I've also been asked, "Gwen, why don't you sit up on the platform at church?" The answer is simple: I feel that my place is in the audience with the people. I sit near the back, always in the same seat, and the ushers know where I am. Because people come up to me or are brought to me, sitting closer to the front would be a distraction. Recently a lady came to me and said she had breast cancer. She handed me a note that said, "I trust your prayers, Gwen. Just pray for me." I found her after the service and had prayer with her. It always amazes me that people are drawn to me, thinking I am so strong all the time and that I have answers for them. I am thankful for that confidence and I respect their trust—but I know where my strength and wisdom come from. Thank the Lord, I can direct them to the same Source—Jesus Christ and the Word of God.

People are lonely and needy, and many want just a touch, a hug, a smile, a prayer. I've had people say to me, "Gwen, when you hugged me last week, it meant so much." I am always honored to know that my hugs are so meaningful because by nature I am a "hugger." I respect the people who come to me because many of them are going through almost unbelievable adversity in their lives.

I want to emphasize the importance of the Word in my life. I always kept my Bible close, whether it was in the hospital, at home, or in my travels. You see, I have been asked over and over, "How do you do it, Gwen? How can you endure so much and still walk strong and stable?" Well, it has been a progression because I am just a normal woman who has asked of God and received from God. It's that simple, really. I love it when my children tell me, "You're a mother who is strong in prayer and in the

Word," because I can turn right around and tell them, "And *you* can be just as strong!" That is the message I want to get out to everyone I touch: Jesus loves you and He can be trusted. Believe His Word and accept it as *good news for you!*

The latest avenue of ministry the Lord has opened up to me is travel—I accompanied David to Europe where he did ministers' conferences and I found that I love overseas ministry more than I could have imagined. The hearts of the people are so hungry for the Word of God and the meetings were amazing. This time the Lord didn't allow me to stay in the background, so I asked Him for wisdom to minister to the women when I was asked to do so. In Helsinki, Finland, I spoke to a group of women and I was almost overwhelmed by their cordiality and generosity of spirit. When I walked into the room, they all stood until I sat down, a new experience for me. It was their way of honoring me and it was special and sweet.

— ❦ —

This is a new season of my life and I am looking forward to more trips abroad. David was fully engaged as pastor of Times Square Church for twelve years, but the Lord has brought together anointed men and women to help carry that load, so he is free to travel more. Recently I asked him, "When are we going back to Europe?" One of the joys of my heart was seeing how God used my husband in ministry to others. As a pastor in New York City, he ministers the Word with love and concern to his own congregation with great anointing. Over in Europe, however, that dimension was enlarged as he reached out to other pastors and their wives with compassion. So many of them were discouraged with their churches and some were even ready to give up on their marriages. David taught them under a strong anointing of the Holy Spirit and you could see them drinking of the Word and becoming stronger. As they put their burdens over on Jesus, miracles began to happen. Praise God for the power of the Word.

Walking with the Lord through the years has taught me many things. I have learned that women everywhere face similar challenges and trials. While I am certainly no expert, I am more convinced than ever that God cares for each one of us *personally.* He is always near, whether you can feel Him or not. He is loving and longs to walk hand in hand with us through *every* circumstance of our lives, good and bad, difficult and easy. He's a good and caring Father and *He never changes!*

Many people ask us about our children and their families. Our two sons and two daughters grew up in the shadow of a well-known father, and even though they loved him deeply and respected him highly, they all wanted to find their own place in God's harvest field and maintain their individuality. I have watched our sons mature into stalwart men of God, establishing Christian homes and ministering in their own callings. I have watched each of our daughters wage a valiant battle with cancer and win—through medical science and the power of Jesus Christ in their lives. All four children have godly spouses and we are happy and proud and very, very grateful for them all.

I have no idea what doors the Lord will open for David and me next. David continues to preach regularly at Times Square Church and he maintains his office there. We still have our apartment in New York City near the church but we also have a place outside the city where we can go when we need to. David takes long walks in the woods and fields surrounding our home and I love to dig in the soil and plant flowers. It's a quiet place where we can relax and regroup. As the psalmist David wrote, *our souls are restored as He leads us beside the still waters.*

Right now we are happy and fulfilled. No matter how small a step of obedience I take, God gives me wonderful rewards. Because of the unity David and I have in our hearts, we enjoy loving children and grandchildren, devoted friends, exciting travels, fruitful ministry and most of all, a closeness to the Savior that provides meaning to all the rest. When I reach out to others, He gives me new partners in prayer, and joy unspeakable. He requires so little from me yet He gives *so much.*

I am blessed! I am loved! And by His grace, I live one day at a time—*abiding in His strength.*